FALSE INTIMACY

UNDERSTANDING THE STRUGGLE OF SEXUAL ADDICTION

DR. HARRY W. SCHAUMBURG

NAVPRESS

BRINGING TRUTH TO LIFE
NavPress Publishing Group
P.O. Box 35001, Colorado Springs, Colorado 80935

The Navigators is an international Christian organization. Jesus Christ gave His followers the Great Commission to go and make disciples (Matthew 28:19). The aim
of The Navigators is to help fulfill that commission by
multiplying laborers for Christ in every nation.

NavPress is the publishing ministry of The Navigators.
NavPress publications are tools to help Christians grow.
Although publications alone cannot make disciples
or change lives, they can help believers learn biblical
discipleship, and apply what they learn to their lives
and ministries.

The actual text of *False Intimacy* was written by Stephen
and Amanda Sorenson.

Some of the anecdotal illustrations in this book are
true to life and are included with the permission of the
persons involved. All other illustrations are composites
of real situations, and any resemblance to people living
or dead is coincidental.

All Scripture in this publication is from the *Holy Bible:
New International Version* (NIV). Copyright © 1973, 1978,
1984, International Bible Society. Used by permission of
Zondervan Bible Publishers.

Schaumburg, Harry W.
    False intimacy : a biblical understanding of sexual
    addiction / Harry W. Schaumburg.
        p.   cm.
    Includes bibliographical references.
    ISBN 0-89109-711-2 : $10.00
    1. Sex addicts—Religious life. 2. Sex addiction—
Religious aspects—Christianity. 3. Intimacy (Psychology)—Religious aspects—Christianity. 4. Sex
addicts—Rehabilitation. 5. Sex addiction—Treatment.   I. Title.
BV4596.S42S33   1992
241'.66—dc20   92-31970
                                                     CIP

Printed in the United States of America

FOR A FREE CATALOG OF
NAVPRESS BOOKS & BIBLE STUDIES,
CALL TOLL FREE 1-800-366-7788 (USA)
or 1-416-499-4615 (CANADA)

Contents

To
Harry and Elizabeth Schaumburg

My denial of my sin protects, preserves, perpetuates that sin!
Ugliness in me, while I live in illusions, can only grow the uglier.

—*Walter Wangerin, Jr.,* Reliving the Passion

Acknowledgments

Over thirteen years ago I began ministering to my first incestuous family. At that time very few people knew about sexual abuse and sexual addiction. I had no clue about the journey I was beginning. That very first family and the many clients and patients who have followed have taught me a lot about sexual abuse and the struggle of sexual addiction. I am grateful to the countless men and women who have shared their lives as we shed tears together and grew in our conviction of the goodness of God.

I am grateful for the many writers, teachers, and friends who have influenced my thinking and my life. Standing alone is the influence of Dr. Larry Crabb. His teachings have profoundly shaped my views of God and counseling. The impact of his ministry has significantly set the direction of this book.

On a cold February in Indiana, one man more than any other had the courage to tear into my life and show me the arrogance of my heart. Dan Allender's "bold love" created in me a passionate hunger for God that made this book worth writing.

My sons, Aaron and Nathan, have all too frequently been turned away as their father hammered away on the keys of the computer. Their sincere patience and understanding helped keep me on task.

My wife, Rosemary, has strengthened and encouraged me by offering the joy of genuine intimacy. The endless hours spent writing this book have kept us both from what we so deeply enjoy. Our shared conviction that I should write this book made the burden lighter.

Lou Porder is a friend who willingly gave valuable feedback. I am indebted to Stephen and Amanda Sorensen for their valuable contribution to this project. Traci Mullins, my editor, has continued to believe in this project and encouraged me by her faith that some day it would be finished. Thanks to her and NavPress for their patience, endurance, and faith in me.

CHAPTER

❖ 1 ❖

What Is Sexual Addiction?

Tony, a young college student, had been adopted at age seven. He had never felt fully accepted by his adoptive family because he didn't resemble his new parents and because later on they had a natural child.

In high school, Tony started masturbating and looking at pornography to give him a good feeling and ease the loneliness.

But the loneliness continued to haunt Tony as he entered college. The more he struggled academically, the more he used pornographic magazines and masturbation to alleviate tension.

After a while he needed a greater "high," so he began calling 900 "Dial-a-Porn" numbers. "This really met a need in my life," he later told me. "Those conversations helped me feel less lonely."

❖   ❖   ❖

One afternoon a woman in her early thirties called me and described for ten minutes how she would compulsively pick up men. "I've been with at least three hundred men, most of them total strangers," she recounted. "I spend a large portion of every day meeting men who are willing to have sex with me. It doesn't matter whether they are young or old, clean or dirty. I just want to have sex with them." Then she told me that she had often been beaten up, raped, or robbed by the men she picked up.

"Do you think it's possible," she asked tearfully, "that someone who will have sex with me will also love me? I'm not sure I can get help. I feel out of control, but it's the only way I can be loved—even though I know those men don't really love me. But I can't give up being 'loved.'"

The fourth and final time she asked if she'd ever be loved, she hung up. I never heard from her again.

❖   ❖   ❖

Stephen started to masturbate in high school. In seminary he progressed to pornography and frequently rented X-rated movies in hotel rooms when he traveled on church business. He married a fine woman, began raising three children, and enjoyed his pastoral duties.

As time passed, however, stresses increased. In his mid-thirties, Stephen began using Monday, his day off, to cruise the city and pick up prostitutes.

"I use prostitutes as a way of relaxing from the rigors of ministry," he said. "I deserve it after working very hard the rest of the week."

❖   ❖   ❖

What do these people have in common? They are *sexually addicted*. This addiction occurs throughout all classes of American society. People from all walks of life—Christians and nonChristians, rich and poor—tenaciously pursue sexual behaviors in order to help alleviate their relational pain and make themselves feel good, satisfied, and in control.

Fueling this behavior is a growing market for sexually oriented goods and services that supply the demand. Motel rooms often provide X-rated movies as a "service." Escort services abound. Nearly every hero or heroine featured in television soap operas is sexually involved with someone. Neighborhood stores rent and sell pornographic magazines and videos. Child sexual abuse is all too common, as are stories of religious leaders who "fall."

Not surprisingly, people have struggled with sexual issues and problems from earliest times. The Bible, for instance, records numerous examples of people who committed sexual sins, although we have no way of knowing whether they were sexually addicted. Shechem, the son of a heathen ruler, raped Dinah, the daughter of Jacob (Genesis 34:1-2). Temple prostitutes regularly solicited business as part of the religious rites of the nations surrounding Israel (Deuteronomy 23:17). Amnon forced his sister Tamar to have sexual relations with him (2 Samuel 13:1-21). Samson spent the night with a prostitute (Judges 16:1). King David chose to watch a naked woman bathe and, consumed with lust, had an extramarital affair with her and then had her husband killed (2 Samuel 11:1-17).

Opinions vary widely on what causes sexual addiction and how to treat it. In the Bible, God sets forth clear boundaries for sexual activity and emphasizes people's need for repentance and salvation from sin. Critics of this teaching argue that the Bible's view of sin ignores the influence of family dysfunction and other factors in the development of sexually addictive behavior. Mental-health professionals debate whether sexual addiction is a disease over which sex addicts have no control or the result of choices influenced by sin. So first we must confront the fundamental question, What is sexual addiction, and how does it manifest itself?

WHAT IS SEXUAL ADDICTION?

As we look at a description of sexual addiction, let's begin with the range of normal sexual responses within a marriage relationship. Think of sexual behavior as being on a continuum:

Sexually   Sexually
Disinterested   Interested

In the normal experience of sexual relations, both spouses experience times when they are interested or uninterested. Typically, one spouse is interested while the other is temporarily uninterested.

A number of factors influence a spouse's level of sexual interest, such as physical appearance, emotional mood, fatigue, or resentment.

For example, picture a married couple who hasn't made love in several days sitting on the couch watching television. The husband looks at his wife and is sexually attracted. He moves closer to hold her hand and place his arm around her. As he begins to kiss her, she feels distracted from the television show and expresses only mild interest compared to his. So he remains where he is but doesn't kiss her anymore. Later, they may come closer together on the continuum of interest and make love.

Farther out along the continuum, a person can move beyond relatively fulfilling sexual relations in a marriage toward some level of sexual tension. This divergence can be illustrated on the following continuum:

| Sexually Repelled | Sexually Disinterested | Sexually Interested | Sexually Engrossed |

The person who is sexually repelled has moved beyond the natural cycle of increasing and decreasing sexual interest and developed a "take it or leave it" attitude—or has even lost *all* interest in sex to the point of personal revulsion. Barring medical reasons, this person is dealing with other relational issues that are impacting his or her sex life. These could include: loss of emotional satisfaction in the marital relationship, previous negative sexual experiences, anger and resentment, or stressful circumstances.

The person who is engrossed in sexual relations, on the other hand, desires frequent sexual relations. In a dating situation or marriage relationship, the sexually engrossed person—typically a man—will pressure his partner to have sex. Such pressure may be uncomfortable, even to the spouse who willingly makes love. The discomfort will increase if she feels that he is having sex more for his own pleasure than to enjoy genuine intimacy with her. As she becomes emotionally ambivalent, she will often move toward becoming sexually repelled.

Table 1.1 describes five people who are facing varying sexual issues. Clearly, persons A and C are sexually addicted, according to how we'll define sexual addiction later. The others face sexual issues and are grappling with what I will call *false intimacy*.

TABLE 1.1. Sample Profiles of Individuals Struggling with Sexual Issues

Person A	Sex: Male Age: 43 Education: College, seminary, doctoral candidate Marital Status: Married nineteen years, infrequent sexual relations with wife, lack of closeness, three children with one in college Sexual Issues: Hires prostitutes one to three times per week, masturbates, buys pornography, visits topless bars, has had three affairs, is a sexually transmitted disease carrier, was arrested for solicitation
Person B	Sex: Female Age: 36 Education: College graduate, certified elementary-school teacher Occupation: Homemaker Marital Status: Married thirteen years, loss of sexual interest, conflicted relationship with spouse, two children (one a preschooler) Sexual Issues: Sexually abused as a child, is sexually dysfunctional with husband, masturbates five or six times per month, reads one to two romance novels per month, watches soap operas daily
Person C	Sex: Male Age: 23 Education: Completed three years of college Occupation: Assistant manager of restaurant Marital Status: Single, broken engagement Sexual Issues: Daily phone sex costs more than $600 per month, masturbates two to three times per day, frequently uses pornography
Person D	Sex: Female Age: 27 Education: In third year of college, 4.0 average, business major Occupation: Striptease dancer, part-time student Marital Status: Divorced, sexually active with current live-in boyfriend Sexual Issues: Raped, had incestuous relationship with father for seven years, has been sexually active with numerous boyfriends since ninth grade, was arrested for prostitution five years ago, has had two abortions

(continue table on next page)

Person E	Sex: Male Age: 38 Education: College graduate Occupation: School teacher Marital Status: Remarried, blended family, sexually active with wife one to three times per week, occasional marital discord Sexual Issues: Sexually abused by older neighbor boy three times at age seven, experienced brief period of impotency with first wife, hires a prostitute each year at state convention, rents X-rated videos approximately every other month

Let's define some terms we'll be using throughout this book.

Perfect intimacy: This refers to the pre-fallen relationship Adam and Eve shared. Naked and unashamed, they joined sexually and relationally with the fullest of pleasure, without hesitation or a hint of self-doubt.

Real intimacy: This is the sexual and relational intimacy two spouses share within their committed, loving marriage. Self-doubts exist, but the couple communicates together and enjoys each other relationally and sexually. Given the reality of a world of imperfect relationships, both partners face disappointments. Within the enjoyment of real intimacy, both partners experience fear of being exposed, fear of abandonment, fear of loss of control, and fear of their respective sexual desires. In their sexual expression, both are dependent on and open to what the other spouse will do.

False intimacy: This is essentially a self-created illusion to help a person avoid the pain inherent in real intimacy. False intimacy can be as slight as a husband who looks at his wife and imagines her having lovely, long brown hair. Something much deeper is reflected in his imagination. Expressed simply, he desires more than he has and demonstrates that he senses something is missing. False intimacy is always present in sexual addiction.

Here is a complete continuum of intimacy and dysfunction:

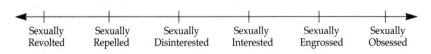

| Sexually
Revolted | Sexually
Repelled | Sexually
Disinterested | Sexually
Interested | Sexually
Engrossed | Sexually
Obsessed |

A person who is sexually revolted has a lifestyle of sexual repulsion. Sex for this person is consuming, for it must be avoided at all costs. A person who is sexually obsessed, on the other hand, lives for sexual pleasure. Sex is again consuming, for it must be obtained at all costs.

Let's look at several illustrations.

Sharon, a successful middle manager, dresses in business suits. Competent and organized, she is ready to handle any situation presented to her. Currently divorced, she has rarely enjoyed sex. During her marriage, she faked orgasms to please her husband. During sex, her mind either wandered or she felt repulsed by the thought of being touched sexually. When she finally shared her feelings honestly with her husband, he left her and remarried.

Now that she is single, Sharon often thinks about sex and finds it disgusting and repulsive. As she did in her marriage, she often finds herself avoiding contact that might lead to sexual relations. Men find her physically attractive, but when they approach her Sharon's response is limited to flirting.

Sharon is afraid of intimacy, of being close, of being sexual, and of losing control in a way that might result in further relational pain. On the surface, she seems to be sexually revolted, but sex doesn't actually consume her. For the most part, she is hiding in the security of false intimacy—as she relates to herself, to others, and to God.

John, thirty-four and single, masturbates as often as three or four times a day. He is moving toward sexual obsession. When he isn't masturbating, he is sexualizing the women in the office, planning to masturbate, or thinking about an X-rated video he saw the evening before. Often he turns in work late, misses meetings, or is late for work because of his masturbation. His problems at work are growing. He has received his last warning for late arrival.

Gail, twenty-six and single, is a secretary who began masturbating as a "source of comfort." Three years ago, she started having affairs with married men at the office. They want to be with her, which she likes, but they don't want emotional involvement, which suits her fine because that's what she fears most. She is moving toward sexual obsession but is relationally uninterested.

What do these people have in common? *They are all involved in false intimacy.* For them, their location on the continuum defines varying levels of sexual interest, sexual activity, and deviation from real intimacy. But regardless of where they fall along the progression, their goals are the same. Each wants to avoid the pain of real intimacy and obtain a sense of relational satisfaction—even if it's counterfeit—through false intimacy. Their motives are strong and rarely analyzed, which can lead to extreme behavior, many risks, and destructive consequences.

How irrational and out of control can a person become in the pursuit of satisfaction and the avoidance of relational pain? A behavioral phenomenon called "autoerotic asphyxia," originally thought to be a form of suicide among teenagers, gives us some idea. In this condition, a person shuts off his or her oxygen supply while masturbating or having sexual relations. The purpose? Intensified orgasm. The consequences of misjudgment? Death.

Sexual addiction is the term commonly used to describe sexual obsession. A sex addict is willing to be destructive to self and others, even breaking the law if necessary, to achieve sexual pleasure. However, we must not assume that sexual addiction is an attempt to find real intimacy. In actuality, it's an avoidance of the pain often caused by real intimacy. In effect, a sex addict creates a pseudo relationship with something or someone who can be controlled, such as a picture, an actor on the video screen, or a prostitute.

Once we understand that the primary goal of sexually addictive behavior is *to avoid relational pain*—essentially, to control life—we can begin to uncover the core problem. Sexual addiction occurs when individuals reach a level of sexual activity that they feel they can no longer control. As addicts become obsessed with sex, they are in danger of deeply misusing it, and at some point they lose control over their sexual behavior while trying to gain control over relational pain.

CORE ISSUES IN SEXUAL ADDICTION: NOT JUST AN ADDICT'S PROBLEM

It's misleading to look at the continuum, particularly the obsessive end, and rather pharisaically think or say, "I may at times be engrossed with sex, but never to the point of becoming a sex addict." Instead of simply examining our behaviors to see if they are destructive or out of control, each of us needs to identify which factors move us anywhere along the line of deviation.

For example, when my wife lacks interest in making love with me, how do I respond? If I casually dismiss my own resentment, however slight, that buried emotion might push me into some form of emotional and/or physical withdrawal.

What about when we decide to use sex as an attempt to relieve the tensions of a demanding day rather than as an expression of love? Plowing through difficult tasks that remind us of our inadequacies may motivate us to approach our spouse with the subtle and perhaps unconscious motivation that says, "Come on, make me feel better about myself — respond!"

As we look at the core issues of sexual addiction, the similarity between the sex addict and the person who uses sex to relieve stress or who withdraws when his spouse isn't interested in having sexual relations is striking. Placed in that situation, some of us may pout; others may masturbate, move away from relationships, read pornography during out-of-town trips, or rent X-rated movies in hotel rooms. Regardless of whether these behaviors in and of themselves can be excused as harmless, they are still the result of a desire to use false intimacy to meet certain internal goals — often the same goals as those of the sex addict!

Internally, each of us is committed to avoiding relational pain. In the right context, this desire to avoid pain is actually a healthy response. But as we diverge from real intimacy, our commitment to avoid being hurt may lead us into the destructive, out-of-control behaviors that help define sexual addiction. As we pursue the goal of constructing our own reality through the illusion of false intimacy, the further we move from the reality in which God has placed us and calls us to live, the more we create our own "insanity." And the more we embrace what is false, the less we care about what is good and loving—and the more we are captive to the desire to create a sense of control over our circumstances.

But no matter how far we move from what is real, we can't escape who we are, who God is, and the reality of other people. The sex addict believes that escape from reality is essential, yet recognizes on another level that such an escape is only temporary. Thus the sex addict faces torment of the soul, guilt, and shame.

Most professionals agree that sexual addiction exists when a person practices sexual activity to the point of negatively affecting his or her ability to deal with other aspects of life, becomes involved in other relationships—whether real or through fantasy—and becomes dependent on sexual experiences as his or her primary source of fulfillment. Simply put, a person demonstrates sexually addictive behavior when he or she is preoccupied with a mood-altering experience in which sexual behaviors have become uncontrollable regardless of the consequences to health, family, and/or career.

The common, popular definition of sexual addiction includes the following four evidences.

Compelling and Consuming Behavior
Sex addicts think and plan their lives around sex. Interestingly, a sex addict is often described as someone who feels an urge or "command from within" to engage in certain sexual behavior. That urge contradicts rational considerations.

A sexually addicted person becomes fully absorbed with sex, for it becomes the greatest need—not the greatest desire. Sex is wanted, demanded, and will be pursued at any cost. Issues such as whether the sex is fulfilling, the partner is attractive or "safe," the pornographic pictures are just illusory, or even if a partner is of legal age, aren't as significant as gaining sexual pleasure.

Behavior Leading to Negative Consequences
Increasingly, the AIDS epidemic is instrumental in making people aware of one negative consequence of sexual addiction. People worldwide acknowledge that sexual behavior can be negative because of the consequence of various sexually transmitted diseases. Other consequences may include: loss of career, reputation, spouse, friends, and

family; financial ruin; legal penalties; court intervention; shame; and continued inability to share in intimate relationships.

Out-of-Control Behavior
Lacking "willpower," addicts feel unable to stop craving, using, thinking about, or caring about sexual behavior even when they know their behavior is harmful and want to stop.

Denial of the Behavior's Seriousness
Sex addicts often deny that their behavior is out of control and that bad experiences are occurring as a result of the addictive behavior. Someone who uses prostitutes may say, "I just need more sex than others, and my wife will have to accept that." The date rapist may say, "She really wanted it as much as I did." The student may say after a sex orgy, "What's wrong with a little fun? After all, no one got hurt." The person addicted to pornography may say, "Everyone buys it—why shouldn't I?"

At the same time, sex addicts often loathe themselves. Sexually addicted individuals have said to me: "I'm a horrible person." "Who would ever love me, a pervert?" "I don't deserve anything." "If people only knew, I'd be tarred and feathered." These persons can struggle with extreme guilt and depression, even to the point of entertaining suicidal thoughts. They live in fear of being discovered and losing everything—family, reputation, money, career, and so on.

I propose that the definition of sexual addiction needs to be expanded beyond the terms commonly used. It is true that sex addicts tenaciously pursue sex as the primary source of their self-fulfillment, and that their sexual behaviors feel out of control. It is true that they are hurting, fearful, riddled with shame, and at times feel that life is hopeless. But I believe that sexual addiction is a symptom of a far deeper problem.

C. S. Lewis wrote, "The process of living seems to consist in coming to realize truths so ancient and simple that, if stated, they sound like barren platitudes."[1] At the risk of offering a barren platitude, I suggest that sexual addiction primarily stems from *the sinfulness of the human heart and a reluctance to be in a passionate, dependent relationship with God*.

The *solution* to sin, however, is not as simple as some Christians make it sound. Often, Christians tend to dismiss complicated problems easily with an exhortation to "trust in God." As we'll see in later chapters, that's far from the point I'm making here.

Sexual addiction is a complex problem with multiple causes and far-reaching consequences. It results when a person becomes dependent on sexual experiences to achieve a sense of personal fulfillment. A person who feels that life isn't fulfilling, who experiences disappointment in intimacy, who loses hope, and who lacks self-confidence is a candidate to be enticed into sexual addiction. The force of the allure goes far beyond sex to the depths of the heart, where the deceitfulness is beyond most people's comprehension.

Few of us have the courage to enter this subterranean world of the human heart. Several tiers below the surface is a pervasive, integral force that demands the right to avoid pain and experience self-fulfillment. This self-centered energy is the very essence of what the Bible calls "sin."

Some people use sexually addictive behavior often, and in ways that are destructive, out of control, and perhaps illegal. This level of sexual addiction, which may involve such behavior as rape and child sexual abuse, has received much attention in books and articles and fits into the classic definition of sexual addiction. But the pursuit of sexual fulfillment and the avoidance of relational pain can be far less public and overt. For instance, a person might be pursuing false intimacy in a marriage relationship without ever questioning his or her motives or behavior. Normally when a couple has sex it is pleasurable for both partners. However, if one partner uses sex simply as a means of relieving stress rather than expressing love and intimacy, he or she is simply using the spouse to fulfill egocentric needs. Unable to deal with real intimacy, this person vows to control the sexual relationship and thus create a sense of feeling safe.

The pastor I mentioned at the beginning of this chapter who picks up prostitutes is at greater risk of obvious consequences than the man having impersonal sex with his wife. The pastor may contract AIDS, lose his church, and be divorced by his wife on the grounds of adultery. However, in some respects the man having impersonal sex with his wife isn't all that different from the promiscuous pastor. Although the behavior they exhibit may differ greatly, the same internal motivations are at work in both men.

The point is, the issue of sexual addiction is more than just the bizarre stories of out-of-control people who use sex in extreme ways. All of us need to look at who we are and how we relate to others. Even if we don't have destructive sexual problems, we may be using sex for the wrong reasons.

The logic of the continuum comes into play when we recognize that using sex inappropriately to meet our deep internal needs can lead to increasingly destructive behavior and have a progressively damaging effect on our ability to function in personal relationships and grow spiritually in our relationship with God.

As we'll see in the next chapter, there are many different types of sexually addictive behaviors. The key point to recognize here is that *sexual addiction isn't just an issue of sex or even of external behavior: It's a byproduct of loneliness, pain, the self-centered demand to be loved and accepted regardless of the consequences, and a loss of vital relationship with God.*

Ralph shamefully described his patterns of chronic masturbation and sexual fantasies to a counselor. He then added, his voice grating with pain, "All I wanted was to be held in someone's strong, loving arms." He longed for intimacy and chose to act in specific ways to get some semblance of what he craved. Sexual addiction is a byproduct of intense, unmet needs, coupled with the demand for fulfillment and control of relational pain independent of God. These needs and demands set up the internal and external dynamics of sexual addiction. Let's look at them more closely.

INTERNAL DYNAMICS OF SEXUAL ADDICTION

When a person demonstrates sexually addictive behavior, certain internal dynamics are always present. Internally, a sexually addicted person demands that life provide an illusion of reassurance and predictability by getting rationalized, self-centered physiological and relational relief and revenge from the intensity of relational pain and shame by avoiding intimacy. Let's break down this definition.

The Internal Nature of Sexual Addiction

Why does one addict who is a childhood sexual abuse victim move toward compulsively acting out sexual behaviors with nameless people in a public rest room, while another victim of similar circumstances loses sexual desire and has a difficult time functioning sexually in a loving marital relationship? Both people are reacting to fear, to discomfort, and to their woundedness, but for some reason they move in entirely different directions. One engages in strange sexual acts with strangers; the other is uncomfortable with the intimacy of sex. Neither of them would understand the other's sex life, because much more is going on internally than can be understood by external behaviors.

What *is* going on inside the addict's mind and heart? What are the motivations? Why do they manifest themselves in particular behaviors? If, as the Bible says, a person's external behavior is an extension of the inner person, then an accurate understanding of sexual addiction must begin with an understanding of that inner person.

Sometimes sin exists in a person's mind without ever surfacing in behavior. For instance, a man may frequently peruse lingerie sales flyers, fantasizing about the models. The material isn't necessarily sexually explicit, yet he is sexualizing the people in the ads. Consequently, this man might sexualize women in a room who are just talking together. In one respect, he hasn't done anything externally; he's "just looking." But from a biblical perspective, he is committing the sin of lust, which often drives people toward other sinful and more overtly destructive behaviors.

The Demand that Life Should Satisfy Our Needs

Sex addicts typically justify their actions and believe their needs must be met. This belief, in turn, becomes a conscious or unconscious demand. "What I need and want," the typical sex addict thinks, "I have to have. My desires need to be fulfilled if my life is going to be worth living. I don't want to feel rejection. I want to be appreciated. Life should deliver the benefits I desire."

The Illusion of Reassurance and Predictability

The addict comes to believe that "if the situation I set up happens, I'll be somebody. I'll be fulfilled. I'm the one who can define what will bring me fulfillment or prevent pain." If the sexual situation provides the benefits that the addict wants and demands, there is a reassurance that he or she has the ability to make that situation happen anytime.

In this way, the addict gains reassurance that life in general is tolerable. If I think I'm pulling the strings, then I can view life as predictable and safe. In effect, the sex addict creates an illusion that brings some fulfillment and definitely less relational pain—in the short run.

After nine months of treatment, a pastor who had a large, successful ministry and a serious sexual addiction observed:

> My ministry was an addiction. It wasn't destructive; I was building a ministry, and people's needs were being met. But the function of the ministry in my life was addictive, just like when I got together with prostitutes. I pursued both with the same tenacity. To have things go well in the ministry did the same thing for me as being with a prostitute regularly.

This pastor had to conquer both addictions. One was an obviously immoral obsession, easily condemned as sinful; the other was a form of workaholism, producing continuous praise and accolades. But he used them both to create the same illusion of reassurance and predictability.

The Habit of Rationalizing Behavior

To create the illusion of intimate relationship, the addict begins to do things that are inconsistent with previously accepted personal standards and values.

For example, lusting after a woman pictured in an intimate apparel catalog is contrary to what God wants a Christian man to do and be, but he may choose to do it anyway. Gradually his standards and values will erode, and his behavior may shift out of a gray area into a clearly destructive arena. But by the time that happens, he has developed rationalizations for his behavior. "How can anything that feels good be so bad? This fulfills a need in me. It makes my life fulfilling. Although I know it's against what I really believe, I'm going to keep on doing it—even it may hurt me and others I love."

Such rationalizations, no matter how bizarre, appear logical to the sex addict. Examples I've heard include: "I only masturbate; I don't go to prostitutes." "I go to prostitutes, but I'd never do anything as disgusting as masturbation." "I only go to high-class prostitutes." "I go to prostitutes, but I'd never have an affair with my secretary." "Yes, I do have some guilt and shame, but I've never molested a child."

Self-Centered Behavior

Addicts' actions are self-centered because at the moment they determine to become involved in a sexual act, the persistent drive to become involved in that behavior demonstrates a lack of concern for others. Addicts aren't deeply concerned about the other people who are affected by their actions. Ultimately, meeting their own needs is most important.

The unknowing spouse of an addict who is having sex with others, for example, is put at risk of communicable diseases. During the process leading up to a child's molestation, an addict who molests children doesn't think about the hurt he or she will cause the child. Even after the molestation, when faced with overwhelming feelings of guilt, the addict will not take the steps necessary to stop the addiction. Even the person who uses pornographic material is more concerned with his or her sexual response than the fact that people featured in the movies and/or literature have been exploited. The sex addict may even encourage other people to do things that harm themselves yet cause the addict to feel good.

The sex addict who is sexually involved with another person, whether a spouse or a prostitute, is more focused on receiving than on giving. Consequently, the other person feels used.

This self-centeredness fuels strong feelings of self-contempt in sexual addicts. Some addicts consider themselves "monsters" — evil people who exploit and harm others. Child molesters often look at themselves in the same way that society in general looks at them — with great disgust. Christian sex addicts are likely to add to that perception the belief that they have committed the unpardonable sin and can never be forgiven. Sometimes sex addicts will have genuine remorse, guilt, and concern for their victims. A minister who had sexual relations with prostitutes said to me, "I'm a demon. My life is more defined by evil than good."

Physiological Relief

Orgasmic release brings physical pleasure. As we'll see, most sexually addictive behavior involves orgasm. For the non-addict, life can be enjoyed beyond the experience of sex. The sex addict, however, demands the duplication of a euphoric sexual moment over and over again at the cost of losing family, friends, career, personal well-being, and integrity.

Physical orgasm does provide a welcome rush of adrenaline, but by itself it can only offer the brief illusion of intimacy and belonging. Again, the key to understanding addictive behavior is that sex addicts' demand to have safety, control over relational pain, and satisfaction causes them to behave in ways that defy their own reason and values—often with disastrous consequences.

Opportunity for Revenge

A person who engages in addictive sexual behavior outside of a marital relationship frequently is getting even with the spouse for "being frigid," "not being interested in sex," "not accepting me the way I need to be accepted," or a number of other reasons. One man who came to me for help said, "I feel very angry toward my wife as I drive to the prostitute." Another man, a pastor, said, "When my wife is cold toward me, I always have my secretary."

The sex addict's revenge is also played out toward the object or person who becomes the sexual focus. A subtle, underlying anger says, "You must give me what I need." The situation is a setup. "I bought the magazine; the photos will give me what I need." "I paid you this money; give me the sexual favors I need." "I paid for this call; give me what I need in this conversation." One woman said it this way: "When they pursue me for sex, I feel powerful. Once they are sexually aroused, I can say no and destroy them." Another said, "Being wanted puts the control in my hands."

Sexual language is a tremendous, subconscious indicator of revenge. Men who consider a woman's beautiful appearance to be a threat or a weapon may frequently describe her as "a knockout," "strikingly beautiful," or "dressed to kill." Some men who feel intimidated by a woman's pretty appearance may think that her achievement is a result of sexual behavior. Therefore they believe that if they achieve a level of sexuality with pretty women, they too will gain power and control. If they can't, they consider themselves failures. Then, feeling angry, resentful, humiliated, or shamed, they want to get even with women for what they perceive has been done to them. Through that revenge, they hope to regain a sense of potency or power.

Temporary Relief from the Intensity of Relational Pain

We all experience wrenching disappointments in relationships. Parents don't always treat their children fairly. Friends aren't always loyal. Supervisors at work can make life difficult.

The sex addict chooses to escape the relational pain caused by these and other disappointments by preventing any type of intimacy from occurring. The sex addict wants a quick fix—quick relational relief without the disappointment possible in genuine intimacy. While turning the pages of a pornographic magazine, while in bed with a prostitute, or when having multiple affairs, the sex addict feels that his or her relationships are working and fulfilling.

But these relationships are really self-made, seemingly safe fantasies structured to be what the addict wants them to be. The addict believes in the illusion of control because he or she controls the illusion. "The centerfold will be everything I want her or him to be." "The people I'm having affairs with will be cooperative and make me feel great."

Fantasy seems to be much safer than risking emotions in unpredictable relationships and suffering the pain that real intimacy can cause. For a brief moment, the centerfold or prostitute is enthralled with the sex addict. Acceptance is unconditional. Rejection is not possible. Sex is a conquest—imaginary or real—and abates the terrifying sense of not belonging. For at least a brief moment, fantasies become more real than life. When a man forces his wife to act, dress, or perform in a sexual way, he makes her an object of selfish gratification but creates a fantasy of being the adequate man who handles life with strength.

Managing the Painful Reality of Loneliness

Since the Fall, all of us have experienced loneliness. We live with the constant reality of our separateness from God and each other. Even after we have become adopted children of God through Christ, we still live in an earthly orphanage in a state of separation from God, awaiting His return and all the benefits of His full custody.

The Fall did not diminish our capacity for intimacy; it created a distortion and an agonizing disruption of intimacy. Each of us longs to break through the limitations of our existence into a blissful, unending intimacy with others. Such a dream cannot, however, be fulfilled. So we desensitize our hunger and thirst for the pre-fallen state by preoccupying ourselves with career, family, food, sex, leisure, and other distractions. But no diversion can richly satisfy our souls. Inner emptiness, the result of original sin, lies just below the surface of the illusions we create in order to cope with life.

Sexual addiction is a fantasy the addict creates to cope with inescapable loneliness. The photographers and editors of pornographic magazines know how to sustain the illusion. The hooker knows how to dress and talk to create the illusion. The voice on the other end of the 900 number knows what to say. They know the techniques to tap into addicts' desires and needs. But the payoff is just money. "I know a prostitute doesn't really love or accept me," a patient said to me during a counseling session, "but she pretends she does and I enjoy the illusion. I really know that to a hooker there are only two kinds of men: clean and unclean. Money is really the bottom line." Another patient said, "If I can hook him with sex, I'll have the relationship I need." She then added, "Somewhere there's a man who will want sex and love me — there's just gotta be!"

The fantasies of a sex addict are feeble attempts to gain what only God is capable of giving, which we will experience partially on earth and fully in Heaven. Sexual fantasy can conjure up a perfect world of nourishment, love, generosity, and tenderness. It can fashion an image of what the addict determines is necessary to gain acceptance and self-worth. The self-created hope of something better provides the sex addict with a source of consolation and a feeling of control.

The truth is, however, that when we try to bury the core reality of emptiness, the result is false intimacy, not genuine. When we insist that our needs for intimacy be fulfilled and ignore the reality that loneliness is always present, we get the very opposite of what we're demanding: We're left alone to stare with open eyes at the harsh reality of nakedness.

This occurs because the demand that loneliness be forcibly eliminated from our lives is an act of putting on a false covering, just the way Adam and Eve did in the Garden of Eden. It's easier to justify our worthiness to ourselves, to others, and even to God by hiding behind pretense rather than to move humbly to His forgiveness, groaning as we wait for our eternal covering in Heaven.

Sadly, to try to escape loneliness by following self-made escape routes, including the path of sexual addiction, is to become even lonelier. Sex addicts are constantly in search of sex, not loving intimacy, that will temporarily reduce their isolation. But they are lonely all the time, trapped in the paradox of being terrified of loneliness even as they act in ways that create further loneliness. They are preoccupied with the demand to avoid being alone, to experience intimacy with a person, a photograph, or an image on a screen who will not cause them relational pain. Yet their chosen behaviors create distance from the genuine intimacy for which they were made.

In so many sex addicts' lives, the combination of controlled response, denial of loneliness, and arrogance stretches their lives too thin. The illusion is shattered, often at the point of public exposure when other people see external symptoms of the their internal desperation and deceit.

Sidestepping Legitimate Shame

In normal, dynamic interpersonal relationships, none of us is everything we should be with our friends, family members, or coworkers. Therefore, in every relationship there is a feeling of inadequacy or shame. Sometimes a simple action, however neutral or insignificant, can cause shame. For instance, a person who suddenly trips over his own feet and falls down in a crowded room may feel that others will think he is deficient in some way.

We want to feel confident and in control. Yet we live with some level of pretense, acting like people we really aren't. We hope to impress people sufficiently so they will accept us in the way we deeply desire. We fear being "found out" and losing relationships with others. We conclude that the people we interact with determine our personal value. We trust in the false gods of people who can let us down rather than recognizing that only God can give us ultimate value, experiencing legitimate shame because we don't trust Him as our Father, and choosing to depend on Him to meet our deepest needs for intimacy.

Illegitimate shame is present when we desperately want to be viewed as sufficient, to be loved and accepted in relationships, and yet we move away from genuine intimacy to avoid being known as someone who isn't perfect. Illegitimate shame can make us fear that something harmful will happen to us, that what we hope for in relationships we won't ever be able to experience. In an attempt to avoid feeling illegitimate shame, the sex addict commits shameful actions over and over again.

Anyone who has enjoyed the deep love and intimacy that sex within marriage provides can comprehend the allure of sexual pleasure. However, the intoxication that can result from orgasmic release is but one small facet of sexual intimacy. God created each of us as sexual beings and designed marital relationships to culminate in the union of "one flesh." In the deepest part of our souls, we yearn to be intimate with another—to be both naked and unashamed in the presence of another. Sadly, pursuing sexual behaviors as ends in themselves, as the source of deep fulfillment, ends only in nakedness and shame—before others and before God.

EXTERNAL DYNAMICS OF SEXUAL ADDICTION

The external dynamics of sexual addiction are manifestations of the internal dynamics we just discussed. External dynamics usually take the form of one particular sexual behavior repeated over and over again, but sometimes the pattern involves several behaviors. Sex addicts set limits on what they will or won't choose to do, but those limits can change if the "high" provided by their customary sexual behaviors begins to lose its power. However, sex addicts usually do not jump from one behavior to another because consistent use of the same behavior(s) becomes predictable, giving the addict the desired sense of internal control.

Examples of external addictive behavior vary:

■ A prominent businessman regularly solicits prostitutes, even though he is risking his health, his marriage, his career, and his reputation.

■ A young person masturbates five times a day, altering schedules to make such secretive behavior possible.

■ A woman telephones a 900 number to talk with a man who "understands." At the end of the month, she must pay fifteen hundred dollars—the money she and her husband had set aside for their daughter's college tuition.

My experience has shown that the more that sex addicts rationalize their behavior, the more it progresses along the continuum. In effect, the addict says, "This behavior really doesn't make sense. This illusion isn't working anymore. So I'll try something else to make life more satisfying. I'll make more 900 calls, try to get a better high from a porno booth, or actually see a naked woman dance." Usually, the first time addicts try a new behavior, they anxiously back away from it. But in a sense they're already "hooked" into that new level of behavior, which then becomes more frequent.

In short, *sexual addiction is a complex result of sin and human behavior*. To state simply that a sex addict is immoral is to state the truth without comprehending the complexity of the problem.

In chapter 3 we'll explore the roots of sexual addiction in more detail. But first, let's look more closely at the kinds of sexual behavior that can be defined as addictive.

CHAPTER

❖ 2 ❖

Sexually Addictive Behaviors

S ex addicts vary in their behavioral choices. Many include masturbation along with other behaviors; some detest masturbation.
Some insist on frequenting the same male or female prostitutes
and are meticulous about cleanliness; others have sex with strangers
in dirty, public rest rooms. One sex addict may have multiple affairs;
another may be incestuously involved with a son or daughter but
would never have an affair or molest someone else's child. To further
complicate this issue, not everyone who has an affair, masturbates, or
has even hired a prostitute is sexually addicted.

In addition, extensive use of one behavior may not necessarily mean
that a sex addict will ever use another sexual behavior. A compulsive
masturbator, for instance, may cause himself or herself physical injury
while never considering using a behavior that could adversely affect
another person. Another addict, however, may make indecent phone
calls, masturbate, and go on to become a child molester or rapist.

As we saw in chapter 1, sexual addiction should be defined more
in terms of its function than in terms of the particular behavior involved.
Specific behaviors such as compulsive masturbation, calling 900 sex
numbers, or even rape don't clearly reveal addicts' core problems.
Because addicts choose behavior that helps them find a sense of fulfill-

ment, avoid pain, and make it through a day, a week, or a lifetime, their degree of perversion indicates the intensity of their demand that their goals be satisfied and reflects the extent of unmet internal needs.

❖   ❖   ❖

Larry's perfectionistic father had been cold and distant, refusing to show emotion and communicate one-to-one with his son. Shy and quiet, Larry turned to his mother for encouragement, but she never praised him and frequently brought up his faults in social settings. By age eleven, he had learned that it was dangerous to initiate or maintain an intimate relationship with anyone.

When Larry was ten, his fourteen-year-old sister began sexually molesting him. At first he was frightened, but as he entered puberty he discovered that this sexual contact was pleasurable for both of them. For the first time, he felt affirmed for his expression of feelings. He felt that he could do something right. Deep inside, however, he knew such contact with his sister was wrong.

In seventh grade he began fantasizing over swimsuit ads in Sears catalogs. Within two years he was using his father's *Playboy* issues to fantasize about women and masturbate.

In college, still feeling relationally inept, Larry continued to sexualize women—in class, in the cafeteria, and on the campus lawn. In the spring, he watched girls lounging on the lawn and then masturbated in his dormitory room. Desiring a bigger thrill, he started peeping through the windows of the women's dormitory at night, hoping to get a glimpse of a woman undressing. During his senior year, he increased the risks. He entered the women's dormitory, located unlocked doors, entered the rooms, and watched the women sleeping. Then he'd return to his room and masturbate.

Like every sex addict, Larry had chosen a particular behavior and its accompanying rituals. In return, he received such benefits as the illusion of love, acceptance, power, and control.

❖   ❖   ❖

Larry's case illustrates how sex addicts' behavior may change through the years. The frequency of addictive behavior may increase, along with the risks to addicts' health, careers, families, and financial situations. Some addicts continue to engage in private behaviors—fantasizing, reading pornography, and masturbating—and progress no further. Others begin to victimize people.

Addictive behavior can be separated into two broad categories: "victimless" (nonintrusive) and "victimizing" (intrusive). Although there are particular types of behavior classified under each category, addicts may participate in aspects of both categories of behavior, just as Larry did.

Any sexually addictive behavior—intrusive or nonintrusive—can lead to severe consequences and/or loss of control. Having sex with a prostitute can lead to loss of job or reputation or even infection with the AIDS virus. Masturbation can get so out of control that it costs individuals their job, and might even require surgery to repair physical damage. A spouse may move out and get a divorce, leading to potentially damaging financial or legal consequences.

"VICTIMLESS," NONINTRUSIVE SEXUAL BEHAVIOR
Nonintrusive sexual behavior doesn't directly hurt someone else physically, and may or may not hurt someone spiritually, mentally, or emotionally. However, such behavior does involve a level of indirect victimization.

For example, when a person compulsively reads pornography, no one else is directly hurt during that act. But the models or actors featured in the pornographic magazines, books, or movies are victims of the profit-making, commercial system that dehumanizes them and pays them a fee to perform. The models and actors who sell themselves are attempting to gain attention, career advancement, acceptance, or meet other needs. In the process they lose a deep part of themselves. So each person who purchases or uses pornography is feeding a system that dehumanizes people, although not victimizing them directly.

Here are some of the types of nonintrusive sexual behavior.

Fantasy Sex
Most people fantasize about aspects of their lives—completing college, finding a mate, earning a lot of money, achieving fame and fortune in a new job, or having a family, to name just a few. Fantasy is often motivational, because it allows us to believe and hope in our ability

to achieve certain goals and objectives. People who are not sex addicts can be legitimately motivated to pursue viable tasks or relationships by imagining great accomplishment and satisfaction.

A sex addict, however, uses fantasy to move toward the unreal world of false intimacy rather than toward the real world of accomplishment and intimate, but sometimes painful, relationships.

By definition, fantasy sex is "thinking/obsessing about sexual adventures . . . creating sexualized or seductive atmospheres that you prefer to keep as fantasy and not act on."[1] Not all fantasies are sexual, and not all sexual fantasies indicate sexual addiction. Most of us, for example, have fantasized about men or women. In high school we wished that certain people would ask us out or respond to us romantically. We've seen attractive people on the beach and wished we could get to know them better.

All sexual involvement begins in the mind, and sex addicts' minds play a key role in their addiction. Lust is all too common in our culture today, but sex addicts lust in the extreme. The amount of time and money they spend on sexual fantasy can threaten everything else they hold dear.

An image of sexual fantasy is just that—an illusive image that someone can control, own, and fulfill any time. Sexually addicted people who use fantasy sex have the false freedom to be vulnerable and nurtured without fear, to touch a bit of the bliss of Adam and Eve before the Fall as, naked and unashamed, they delighted in each other's bodies free of self-doubt or self-consciousness. But at its core, *sexual fantasy is a worship of self,* a devotion to the ability of people to fabricate in their minds the solution to what they know is a need and believe they deserve.

As with other addictive behaviors, it's difficult to generalize about addictive fantasy sex and why people use it to meet deep, unmet needs. For instance, two women may read a steamy romance novel. The first one enjoys it but puts it down when her real relationships and responsibilities demand attention. The second one fantasizes about having a relationship with one or more men described in the book, desiring to drink from the fountain of life's pleasures, to be fulfilled sexually and emotionally, to be lifted out of the mundane into the sublime, to have her femininity restored. The first woman is able to read about intimate relationships for enjoyment while remaining able to function fully in the real world. The second, however, uses the fictional fantasy to fuel her unmet desires for intimate relationships and loses touch with reality.

Sexual fantasizing is convenient; it can be done anywhere. Usually performed in seclusion with no possibility of interruption destroying the illusion, sexual fantasizing can include a gracious, imaginary partner—the perfect lover who responds to one's every desire without complaint.

Fantasizing can also take place with a spouse or prostitute, when the person fantasizing is present in body but absent emotionally and often mentally. If we picture the continuum mentioned in the preceding chapter, we can see that sexual fantasy can include aspects of being sexually engrossed without expressing the traits of sexual obsession. Although fantasizing is not always an addiction, the goal is the same: *to create false intimacy and avoid relational pain.*

Frequently, when a person sexually fantasizes alone, he or she masturbates, stimulating the genitals to the point of feeling pleasure or experiencing orgasm. Most psychological literature informs us that masturbation is a common behavior. But to the sex addict, it becomes a frequent, secret part of life that is perceived as necessary to get through the day. It's not uncommon for a sex addict to masturbate three to five times a day, and even as many as ten times a day to the point of physical injury.

The following reflection, while not the actual quotation of a sex addict, communicates in frank terms why even a lack of sexual interest can be a commitment to false intimacy. These comments explain why fantasy is so easily chosen and how it moves a person along the continuum toward becoming engrossed or obsessed with sex:

> When I return home from work, I'm tired. I've battled traffic, been in meetings, and didn't get any exercise. Now I just want to play with the kids before they go to bed, eat something, and relax in front of the television. If the shows aren't great, I'll read a magazine or a novel.
>
> I kiss the kids goodnight and watch a bit of the news. My wife's tired and is going to bed soon. So I sit down and read a novel I picked up in the airport last week. The hero finds himself in this canyon with a beautiful woman who crawls into his sleeping bag.

Even though they must be awfully cramped in there, I'm getting turned on by this illusory, illicit liaison. Yes, my wife is lying in the next room, and she'd probably be happy to make love with me. But I'm not turned on by her right now. I'm turned on by these words marching across the page.

Because, see, if I'm going to have sex with my wife, I'll have to put down the novel, brush my teeth, and find out how she's really doing. And I guess we should use birth control, just in case. Then I'll have to ask what she's thinking about, how her day has gone, whether she bought the new dress after work, and things like that. I'll have to tell her a few things about my day, too, even though I'd rather not think about most of it. I'll have to hold her, caress her, let her know she's important, and undertake an act that I may not be able to consummate. Or, I'll be left feeling that I didn't care enough about her sexual needs. No, I think I'll stick with the marching words on the page and masturbate.

The man in this illustration weighed the alternative to fantasy sex and didn't feel that he was able to "jump through all the hoops." He just wanted to relax and escape the day's pressures. But once such patterns take hold in his life, it may become easier for him to fantasize than to make the effort to be intimate with his wife.

Visual Sex

Visual sex, often performed with masturbation, is mixed with fantasy. Visual sex behavior may include attending strip shows where men and/or women can be seen but not touched, watching sexual activity in booths, and viewing sexually explicit pornography in magazines or films. Actual pornography doesn't have to be present, however, since a sex addict can simply look at a person and mentally undress him or her.

A man might stare at a beautiful woman on the beach and be perfectly content to experience a less-than-perfect relationship with the woman he has been married to for twenty years. Another man might stare at the same woman and long to have sexual relations with her in an attempt to heal his empty soul. When the second man caresses his wife in bed, his mind may be on the beautiful woman of illusion who is always at his beck and call, eager to fulfill his every wish and far away from household routines, miscommunication, and conflicting priorities.

Pornography is another illusion of visual sex, for it involves no kissing, tenderness, softness, or intimacy. It is free from the vulnerability and uncertainty that embrace all relationships as a result of sin's entrance into the world. The compulsive viewer of pornography is physically and emotionally detached. There is little risk of pain. The "relationship" is with dots on a page, with a man or woman who can't be truly touched—with a fantasy. The tragedy of sexual addiction is that the sex addict wants to touch and be touched—literally to be one flesh—but is left only with self.

The escape from intimacy leads to an escape from loneliness through an escape into pornography. Sex addicts who use pornography to escape extreme loneliness are quite different from people who casually read such magazines as *Playboy* or *Penthouse*. Sex addicts have been known to purchase thousands of dollars of pornographic material, to rack up insurmountable debts, and to arrange for second mortgages on their homes so they will have enough money to collect sexually explicit materials.

Carnes' survey of sex addicts showed that 90 percent of the men and 77 percent of the women who responded used pornography as part of their addiction.[2] Carnes further states that there is an extensive, sexual "'cottage industry' with gross annual revenues of somewhere between seven and ten billion dollars. We spend more on pornography in one year than the annual sales of the Coca-Cola corporation."[3]

Verbal Sex

The behavior of verbal sex, in which people may exchange money, occurs when someone talks with someone else—usually a member of the opposite sex—in order to receive sexual stimulation. The most common form of verbal sex is the 900 number, which someone can call for a fee and either listen to a tape or talk sexually with a live person.

But in other situations, no money is required. One sex addict I counseled didn't call a 900 number. Instead, he called his two previous wives and carried out this behavior with them. Still others talk sexually to others at work or during parties, sexually harass people, or "just" tell sexual jokes.

Nicholson Bakker's best-selling novel *Vox* chronicles the lives of two strangers in separate cities who discover each other by telephone. As an ad for the book suggests, this couple "in revealing all, reinvent sex." One of them responds to an ad that has the headlines: ANYTIME AT ALL and MAKE IT HAPPEN. Both people are mutually seduced, since they are each looking for an alternative way to be together without risk.

The man says, "And so the reason I called this line was that the pleasures I'd sought out weren't doing it for me and there was this hope of luck, that I, that there would be a conversation."[4]

A quarter of the way through their phone call, the woman mentions that the call is getting expensive for him. A brief discussion ensues as to how they'll exchange personal numbers. She fears that some unforeseen force will prevent them from finding each other again, such as neither of them writing down the numbers correctly. He expresses real fear that she won't call him back, but she says, "I'm going to call you back. I'm enjoying this. I'm going to call." [5]

Eventually they become convinced that it's too risky to hang up the phone. "All right," the man says, "you convinced me. . . . Really I think two dollars a minute is cheap for this. I need this. I'd spend twenty dollars a minute for this."[6]

Both characters are terrified of losing the false intimacy they've created. As they continue their conversation and share secrets that are safe only with a stranger, the man says, "This is a miracle."

She responds, "It's just a telephone conversation."

"It's a telephone conversation I want to have. I love the telephone."

"Well I like it too. There's a power it has."[7]

Tragically, the couple find false — virtually pornographic — intimacy through the phone lines by sharing sexual secrets. This way of telling secrets seems safe. The stranger listens intently and accepts what is heard. Neither person must face the pain or fear that once they are physically together either of them might be unacceptable to the other.

Physical Sex

Physical sex involves bodily contact between the sex addict and one (or more) person(s) of the same or opposite sex for the purpose of sexually arousing one or both people. Female sex addicts, according to Carnes' research of recovering sex addicts, are more likely to become involved in nonintrusive physical sex than any other types of behavior.

The irony of addictive, nonintrusive physical sex behavior is that it involves human contact yet is similar to fantasy sex in that the sex addict isn't really emotionally involved with partners or committed to their well-being. There's a palpable illusion of intimacy, but no substance. The sex addict has a self-centered focus on "the two becoming one flesh." This type of behavior is called "victimless" because it takes place between consenting adults who willingly choose to participate.

Obviously, from a biblical perspective people who are involved in the following behaviors are breaking God's laws and will suffer consequences:

Prostitution. Soliciting prostitutes is a common physical sex behavior, participated in by people from all walks of life, including Christians. Because of the willingness of both parties, prostitution is not typically considered to be intrusive. Yet it could be considered intrusive, since many prostitutes are only teenagers, runaways, or homeless people. Many are victimized by pimps or by those who purchase their sexual favors.

Addicts who choose this behavior may procure sex from a drug-addicted hooker and/or high-priced male prostitute or simply use an "escort" service. Committing sexual acts with a prostitute is, in certain respects, similar to fantasizing about an imaginary person, for it allows the person paying for sexual favors to create a fantasy with an actual willing, cooperative person. The sex addict pays someone to do specific sexual acts as a way of participating in that fantasy. Sex is all that the addict receives.

Prostitution enables the sex addict to participate in anonymous sex while rationalizing that the money paid for services justifies any demands he makes. Sometimes the fears or inhibitions a sex addict has with a spouse may disappear with a prostitute, further adding to the power of the illusion. One man, typical of many sex addicts I've counseled, told me, "A good prostitute does a good job of selling herself, of convincing me that she really wants me for who I am. Rationally, though, I know that she really doesn't care about me at all." Addicts who appreciate this higher level of fantasy don't want to perceive themselves as demanding the prostitute's sexual favors, and so the most popular prostitutes appear willing and play their illusory parts well.

Another man I counseled routinely visited three prostitutes a week, even though he hated the fact that he did it. (Sex addicts often see prostitutes regularly, not just once a year or on business trips, as some believe.) Married, with two children, he was so afraid of intimacy that he could only make love with his wife when her face was covered by a sheet. So prostitutes — and the anonymous sex they provided — helped him manage the uncertainty. Over time, he realized that he had used the prostitutes to fabricate an illusion of acceptance and security.

Promiscuous sex. Extramarital affairs occur at an alarming rate and cause great confusion, disorientation, and destruction. Frequently sex addicts engage in multiple affairs, using seduction to gain power over others.[8] These nonintrusive affairs take place between mutually consenting adults who may or may not know each other well. Usually some kind of relationship exists between the sex addict and the other person(s). Seldom are affairs just a way in which people obtain anonymous sex.

Sam, a pastor and counselor, is a good example. He showed genuine interest in the marital struggles of Gwen and her husband. Increasingly, Gwen shared the extent of their problems, her depression, and her anger. Sam listened well, showed interest, made supportive comments, and cared for her well-being. "Just call me anytime," he told her. "I could meet you when you're down."

Everything about Sam — his empathy, warmth, caring, and interest — stood in stark contrast to Gwen's husband. One morning Gwen came up to him, leaned on his shoulder, and said, "Please hold me." He did, and they began kissing and fondling each other. From that day on, they extensively kissed and fondled each other whenever they were together. But Sam was exploiting her weakness, her needs, her desires to be held, loved, and supported. He was no longer helping her; he was using her.

When Gwen's husband discovered the affair, he made sure that Sam was removed from the pastorate. Sam, however, continued the relationship in spite of its negative consequences. His addiction to Gwen was so strong that when he came to me for treatment he was seriously considering leaving his wife and children and changing his theology to justify his activities. Only after extensive treatment could he admit that he had been exploitative and end the affair.

❖   ❖   ❖

Engaging in extramarital affairs is the most common nonintrusive physical sex behavior used by sex addicts. However, not everyone who has an affair is a sex addict. In fact, the line between addiction and nonaddiction is hard to distinguish. Indicators of addiction may include having multiple affairs and/or feeling driven to have an affair even though it will lead to awful consequences. A small or moderate amount of challenge increases the addict's sense of power, control, and competence, followed by feelings of pleasure or achievement. Danger and excitement are kissing cousins in affairs. People can become high on their own stress. Excitement is a part of anger and fear. Some sex addicts become addicted to risk-taking sexual behaviors. They enjoy not only the orgasmic release but the stimulation of the risk of danger. Once the behavior is completed, they feel the momentary high of adventure and conquest, having proved their desirability and power.

Numerous one-night stands, group sex, or having multiple sexual encounters with the same person are also included in this nonintrusive physical sex category. Some sex addicts patronize bars, saunas, or massage parlors to locate willing partners. The bottom line, however, is that sex addicts need the security of false intimacy, danger, and anonymity that illicit sexual activity provides. They use it to sustain the illusion that they are accepted.

One married addict in therapy said, "For forty-five years I've never met a woman I didn't try to seduce." The "conquests" included every secretary who had ever worked for him, his wife's friends, store clerks, hotel maids, the family's personal maids, clients, and colleagues. He sought therapy because at age sixty-five he wanted real relationship, genuine approval, and a taste of being loved without the numerous and fabricated encounters with people he knew and with nameless, virtually faceless strangers.

Another man became sexually involved with three women in a couple's Bible study that he and his wife attended. He used his position and natural listening skills to groom the three most needy women into a "caring" relationship that he ultimately used for his sexual gratification. The risk, the control, the power, and the ability to juggle his schedule and make excuses to pull off what he perceived as such a sensational feat provided their own high.

A thirty-two-year-old homemaker with two preschoolers had nine affairs during her five years of marriage. "I couldn't believe that a man accepted me unless we had sex," she told me later. "My mother always told me that being beautiful, physical, and sexual gave me worth and value. So I acted this out, even though I felt dirty and wished I could stop."

A pastor in a southeastern town confessed, "I've had sexual contact with more than one thousand women I've met at beaches, parks, in parking lots, and near rest rooms. I wanted to see if I could get them. It was a game, really."

Object Sex

Sex addicts sometimes use one or more objects to increase pleasure during sexual activity. These objects or fetishes—which could be under-garments, a belt, or a household item—are given sexual significance. Masturbating with objects and dressing in clothing normally worn by the opposite sex are included in this category, as is bestiality—engaging in sexual activity with animals.

Object sex can provide tremendous addictive power. Whereas non-addicted people are typically confused by such behavior, the addict may be addicted to using objects that have become sexualized, even when the objects are disgusting and vulgar. The Bible clearly prohibits object sex.[9]

Don, a young pastor, made great progress during three weeks of in-patient treatment and avoided the fetish of smelling women's soiled underpants. But during the fourth week he went to a laundromat and acted out this behavior again, with great disgust and shame.

Recently a corporation vice president with AIDS was arrested for having sex with young boys. Investigators discovered that he would pay as much as forty dollars for a pair of smelly socks and fecal samples.

Another counselee described having sex with animals countless times, whenever he felt stressed or lonely. "I am having a difficult time," he told me one afternoon. "Every day I have to drive by that field and those animals. It's like I can't help myself. I want to stop and go into the field."

My experience with patients who have been involved in bestiality is quite limited. But other mental-health workers are surprised by the number of sex addicts who are regularly involved in bestiality. Patrick Carnes surveyed sex addicts involved in object sex and found that 31 percent of the men and 23 percent of the women who responded engaged in sexual activity with animals.[10]

INTRUSIVE SEXUAL BEHAVIORS

Simply put, intrusive sexual behavior is sexually related visual or physical contact that is done without permission of the other person. It includes "making inappropriate advances or gestures; touching or fondling others without permission . . . forcing sexual activity on any person including your spouse or partner."[11] In this type of sexual activity, sex addicts involve themselves with someone else against that person's will in order to satisfy their need.

Intrusive sexual behaviors, which involve direct or indirect sexual contact that violates people, usually create some emotional, spiritual, or even physical damage. Rape, for example, causes victims to experience great pain.

However, intrusive behaviors can victimize people even without the victim's awareness of what is taking place. The key issue here is what is in the mind of the sex addict, who may treat victims impersonally without consideration for their spiritual and emotional well-being. Whether through visual or physical contact, the sex addict relates intrusively to another person as if the person has no soul.

For example, a sex addict might deliberately brush a hand against another person's body in a hallway or mentally undress a person during the coffee hour at church. The goal is to fulfill unmet needs without any consideration of how the victim might feel. Certainly the victim, who is probably unaware or uncertain of what is happening, would feel violated and used if he or she knew the other person's lustful thoughts or intent.

Another form of subtly intrusive behavior occurs when a willing sexual partner is unaware that he or she is being manipulated for the partner's sexual gratification. An example of this is when a partner in a position of power and trust—a pastor, counselor, employer, doctor, lawyer, teacher—uses his or her position to violate trust and gain sexual satisfaction, regardless of the partner's willingness.

In our society, people who are certain that intrusive behaviors are occurring may respond with outrage and severe punishment, including legal penalties. But not all intrusive behaviors result in legal consequences. Some intrusive sexual behaviors such as exhibitionism are even considered a bit "humorous" and aren't taken so seriously.

Visual Sex

Voyeurism — "stealing" views of unwilling victims in a variety of situations — is an intrusive behavior in which lust has gone wild due to the addict's internal void. Voyeuristic activities include watching people through binoculars or telescopes, peeping through windows, or undressing someone with the mind's eye.

Voyeurism is intrusive whether or not the victims are aware of being watched. For instance, if a woman turns around and suddenly sees a face at her bedroom window, she obviously experiences intense fear, anger, and confusion. But even if she doesn't notice the face, she is still a victim of someone's lustful and selfish desires.

Men in particular use voyeuristic behavior almost reflexively in what might appear to others to be just a glance or a stare. They retain the images of women and later use those "stolen" images to enhance their fantasies. The issue here is that the women didn't intend to give away their images for purposes of someone's self-gratification. If the women were aware of those sexual images, they'd be highly offended and feel intruded upon and victimized.

Although intrusive visual sex is often excused, it's really a depersonalizing way of using sex to aggressively degrade others and use them as objects.

Exhibitionism is also intrusive. More than just the stereotype of the man with a trench coat, this pattern of sexual exposure includes any type of exhibitionistic behavior — from a person's car, home, or other location. Some sex addicts choose to dress in an extremely provocative manner. Typically, more women than men use this "safer" type of behavior. One reason is that few men ever report such behavior to the authorities.

Some people in therapy have reported that they exposed themselves from high-rise apartment windows where it was difficult for the police to pinpoint the location. The ultimate "high" was when someone else, in turn, exposed himself or herself from a different window.

Verbal Sex

Making obscene telephone calls is an intrusive form of verbal sex, for it verbally assaults unwilling listeners. This is in contrast to nonintrusive telephone calls, in which both parties willingly participate in sexualized conversations. In some cases obscene callers are unable to initiate normal intimate relationships, so they prey on total strangers.

A client of mine used another type of intrusive verbal sex at fast-food restaurants. He'd pull up to the drive-through window, pretending to be collecting his food, and then verbally assault the woman at the window, driving away quickly before anyone could get the license number of his car. Another client intruded on others by telling sexually explicit stories or making sexually explicit comments in front of them.

Physical Sex

A number of intrusive sexual behaviors involve physical contact. These include:

Child sexual activity involves having any physical contact with a minor for the purpose of sexual arousal. Included are incest, sexual molestation of children, graphic sexual talk in front of children, showing children pornography, and viewing child pornography with children. Sadly, child sexual abuse is a major problem nationwide—and occurs in many church families.

Rape, in which a partner—usually someone the rapist knows—is forced to participate in sexual activity, can occur within a marriage when one spouse forces the other to have sexual relations, and in dating situations when one person forces the other to have sexual relations. Sometimes a stranger will sexually attack others at random or after making elaborate plans to stalk specific people.

Exploitation occurs when a person in a position of power and trust—such as a pastor, counselor, lawyer, doctor, employer, or teacher—has sexual contact with someone who believes that he or she won't be used for personal advantage. Regardless of which person initiates the sexual behavior, whether or not both people willingly cooperate in the behavior, and whether or not intercourse occurs, such behavior is always exploitative because of the factors of trust, power, and dependence. A growing number of states are creating laws that make it a felony for someone in a position of power and trust to become sexually involved with a patient or client.

Sadomasochism involves tying up, spanking, or otherwise punishing one partner in order to provide the sex addict with pleasure. Inflicting pain on others seems to contradict the idea of sexual intimacy between a man and woman deeply in love. Sex addicts using this behavior are full of contempt for themselves and the other and are committed to relief and revenge.

Inappropriate touching of someone's body in a room or crowded elevator is also an intrusive behavior. The touching may be as brief as a brush of the hand or as violent as actually grabbing another person's body and then running away.

Impersonal sex within marriage is intrusive because a spouse is used only as an object of gratification. Perhaps a spouse is required to have sex on demand—when, where, and how the partner wants it. Or in some cases a spouse is pressured into committing sexual acts that he or she finds distasteful, or must commit sexual acts with another person while the spouse watches.

SUMMARY

A sex addict who uses any of the behaviors listed in this chapter—mentally, visually, verbally, physically—believes that the other real or imaginary person(s) will relieve his or her inner emptiness. Each time the chosen sexual behavior(s) is used, the addict's emptiness is numbed or temporarily forgotten. But the consequences of the addict's unmet needs and external sexual behavior(s) continue. The emptiness returns, and with it the realization that whatever person or object or picture or video the addict used didn't provide lasting benefits. Then fear, anger, and/or resentment kick in, and the sex addict again must pursue the behavior(s) that he or she believes is essential to well-being and fulfillment.

Sexually addictive behaviors, as we've seen, are symptomatic of internal problems. Each behavior has a function that enables the addict to cope with life. Below the surface, the addict is steeped in desperation and anxiety, fear and shame, and sadness and loneliness. These desperate feelings simply drive the addict to keep the illusion of fulfillment going.

Sexuality used to create false intimacy presents the perfect illusion: limitless capacity for orgasm and superhuman calisthenics, control, the perfect partner, sexual fulfillment on demand, excitement, freedom from conventional restraints, danger, no fear of rejection, no pain of failure, and no disappointments. These unreal expectations further promote false intimacy.

For the sex addict, each external sexual act is a desperate attempt to be involved in a relationship without being truly known and having to take the risks involved in developing real intimacy. In effect, the addict pushes his or her desires for warmth and love to the limits, demanding complete satisfaction without the risk of being hurt. Sadly, such behavior invariably creates far more intense pain than the original pain the addict is trying to escape and/or prevent.

Let's now consider the various internal and external factors that influence a person to develop sexually addictive behavior.

CHAPTER
✦ 3 ✦
What Causes Sexual Addiction?

M any people in our society struggle with a variety of compulsions and the painful loss of control over their actions.
But why do people develop addictive behaviors that bring
them pleasure, invigoration, relaxation, and an escape from the bore-
dom and despair of a fallen world — at the cost of their health, families,
careers, and personal freedom? Whatever we accept as the cause(s) of
sexual addiction will influence both our approach to caring for sexually
addicted people and the steps we take to prevent sexual addiction from
developing.

I don't expect that this chapter or the rest of this book will resolve
the issue of whether addiction is a sin or a disease. Debate on this issue
will likely continue long after this book is out of print! However, I
believe this issue is critical and must be addressed. Although this
brief chapter may stir you to pursue new depths of thinking, it is not
intended to be a comprehensive critique of the recovery movement or
the concept of addiction as disease.

The nature and role of the recovery movement is a highly emotional issue. Many people who have successfully battled addiction
within their respective recovery groups have no other lifeline that will
help to support their sobriety. So it's easy to understand why they

develop evangelistic fervor about the value of such groups. Others at the opposite extreme believe strongly that such recovery groups don't accomplish nearly enough or even mislead those they purport to help.

Regardless of which direction we lean toward personally, we all must honestly acknowledge with great sadness that churches have often been unresponsive to the needs of addicted people, causing them to feel neglected or condemned. Many believers have experienced more love and compassion in a recovery group than in the "fellowship of believers." Without a doubt, recovery groups have "saved" people from the destructive grip of addiction. For this we can rejoice and, facing the scarcity of resources within the church, pray that many more people will experience freedom from the bonds of addiction.

As you read further, please realize that my intention is not to foolishly attack obviously successful approaches to recovery, but to encourage readers to passionately pursue God on a deep level. If people face the nature of their sexual addiction as a result of reading this chapter, I'll be thankful, but I hope they'll go even deeper and develop a greater thirst for God.

After years of working with sex addicts who feel they can't control the starting or stopping of their addictive behaviors, I've concluded that there are no easy explanations for why some people become sexually addicted. The contributing internal and external factors are complex, involving human nature, environment, and sin. Before we explore these specific factors, let's look at two basic models commonly used by mental-health professionals and others approaching sexual addiction: the medical disease model and the biblical model.

THE MEDICAL DISEASE MODEL OF SEXUAL ADDICTION

The central issue in developing a framework for understanding what causes sexual addiction revolves around this question: What are we really dealing with when the "symptoms" of sexual addiction exist?

In 1951 and 1952, an American pioneer in studies of alcoholism at the Yale Summer School of Alcohol Studies, E. M. Jellinek, stated that alcoholism is a progressive and potentially fatal disease. Since that time, the addiction movement has expanded beyond the treatment of alcohol and drug addiction to the treatment of almost any behavior that is excessive—overeating or eating too little, smoking, workaholism, stealing, codependency, compulsive shopping, gambling, chemical abuse, loving too much . . . and the list goes on.

Simply put, a behavior or set of behaviors is now labeled a disease or addiction when a person does it more often than he or she knows it should be done. Ironically, mental-health professionals often view both the addicts and the people hurt by addicts as disease victims who need medical treatment.

Historically, the word *disease* addressed physical disorders such as heart ailments, cancer, and pneumonia. Diseases caused improper functioning of the human body, and the science of medicine dealt with preventing or controlling the damage that a disease could do to the body through inoculations, medications, and surgery. In this framework, emotional and behavioral disorders expressed through feelings, thoughts, and behaviors were not considered diseases.

Today, however, a number of professionals view sexual addiction as a disease. Their medical disease model states that sexual addiction is a behavior that people can't control.

The loss of control over a part or all of a person's functioning is terrifying. For example, the thought of an adult becoming enuretic and having to wear a diaper again seems disgusting, embarrassing, and frightening. If addiction is a disease, then it exists autonomously within a person's life, dictating choices the individual must make to compensate for the disease. This condition makes the addict feel powerless to control the addictive behavior or manage various aspects of life.

Within this framework of the medical disease model, the sex addict could be considered a passive victim who faces the unavoidable loss of control over sexual functioning—in other words, the addiction is a condition in which a normally healthy person becomes unhealthy. At issue, therefore, is how the sex addict becomes "sexually enuretic." It would seem, by the embarrassing, destructive, and frightening qualities of sexual addiction, that no sane person would ever want to become involved in this addiction. Why, for instance, would a man who is a good father, successful pastor, and devoted husband become involved in sexually addictive behaviors? Surely only powerful forces underlying such behavior could produce such tragedy! Pervasive, strong forces certainly *are* at work in the lives of sex addicts. The critical question is, What are those forces?

The concept of sexual addiction as a disease offers real comfort. If I ever become afflicted with the disease of enuresis, I will be comforted by knowing that numerous factors beyond my control have contributed to the development of this disease. I often receive a similar response when counseling spouses of sex addicts. For example, a pastor's wife who discovered that her husband had had multiple affairs comforted herself by saying, "Because he was involved in multiple relationships and his actions obviously contradicted everything he stood for as a father, husband, and pastor, a disease had to be driving him." That eased her pain, since the issues were no longer abandonment, the overwhelming news that she had been betrayed for five years, anger at what he'd done, and so on.

Often sex addicts grab hold of the concept of disease when informing their spouses about their addiction in order to gain acceptance, understanding, and avoid losing their relationships. The desire to discover ways of changing behavior and restoring marital relationships is valid, but I believe this desire should not cause people to avoid what I consider to be the deeper causes of sexual addiction.

Christians often categorize sexual addiction as a "sin" and then define sin as an uncontrollable disease without fully developing the real definition of sin. Part of the difficulty in evaluating sexual addiction in light of sin is that sin *is* uncontrollable. Does this mean we can conclude that sin equals addiction and that addiction equals sin? Are they the same? No. Understanding addiction doesn't always help us to define the characteristics of sin or the approach to cures for addiction. Sin is much more than just unhealthy choices, loss of control, or destructive behaviors—all of which are symptoms of sin.

The essence of sin is *autonomy from God,* a failure to be dependent on Him. Sex addicts don't go from being healthy to unhealthy because of a disease labeled addiction. Their refusal to cling to God as the only Person who can fill their deepest longings and ease relational pain did not originate in a shame-based family but in their shameful, deceitful heart. All of us have such a heart.

The refusal to depend on God as the only source of true fulfillment can be seen primarily in our relationships with one another. One person may demonstrate such symptoms of sin in the heart as unkind words, malice, hypocrisy, deceit, envy, and slander (Titus 3:3, 1 Peter 2:1). These actions can feel uncontrollable and can certainly be destructive. In another person's life, there may be "sexual immorality, impurity and debauchery; idolatry and witchcraft; hatred, discord, jealousy, fits of rage, selfish ambition, dissensions, factions and envy; drunkenness, orgies, and the like" (Galatians 5:19-21).

It's not enough for any of us to change our behaviors or even improve the quality of our relationships with one another. We must develop and strengthen our relationship with God and reflect that relationship in our interactions with other people. A sex addict truly changes when his or her relationship with God changes. Although this may seem simplistic to some, the complexity occurs in what is involved in that change. This is the process that needs to be carefully defined.

THE BIBLICAL MODEL OF SEXUAL ADDICTION

Mental-health professionals agree that there is much to learn about addictions in general and sexual addiction in particular. However, I believe a biblical understanding of sexual addiction, based on God's understanding of us, must be used first to answer questions about who we are and why we do what we do. If we simply "begin" with an explanation of ourselves—who we are and why we do what we do, without beginning with who God is and what He is doing, we will overlook the entire spiritual dimension of addiction.

The Bible, the infallible Word of God, provides a strong framework through which we can understand sexual addiction and "the sin that so easily entangles" us (Hebrews 12:1). We can gain foundational insights into God's character, human relationships, the delights of our sexuality, and the shame of our sin by studying the book of Genesis, which shows the sexual intimacy that existed before the Fall.

The consequences of the Fall on human sexuality are of immense significance in understanding sexual behavior. On the broadest level, the Fall resulted in our maleness and femaleness being threatened. We became naked and ashamed of our sexuality. The Fall impacted all ensuing relationships, and thereby all sexual relationships.

When God created Adam and then Eve, He designed their sexuality and resulting lovemaking to be an expression of perfect intimacy—the antithesis of self-gratification. In Genesis 2:23-25, we read an appealing account of a man and a woman delighting in sexual intimacy:

> The man said, "This is now bone of my bones and flesh of my flesh; she shall be called 'woman,' for she was taken out of

man." For this reason a man will leave his father and mother
and be united to his wife, and they will become one flesh. The
man and his wife were both naked, and they felt no shame.

We see God's acknowledgment that their intimacy was good. In His
creation lay all the fulfillment of intimate sharing and new life. We
sense the unimaginable goodness of God's gift of sexuality, which was
far more than genital pleasure, a remedy for concupiscence, or God's
attempt to control lust. Adam and Eve experienced the incomprehen-
sible joy of being together as one flesh and the pleasure of continual
uninhibited, intimate relationship.

After Adam and Eve disobeyed God, sin tainted what God had
created. The blissful intimacy Adam and Eve had known was lost. Sin
invaded human nature and human sexuality became perplexing. That
is why sexual intimacy today is accompanied by times of deep frustration and increasing numbers of couples who are looking for help with
sexual concerns. Infidelity, sexual dysfunction, and sexual abuse are
frequent issues in counselors' offices, where people seek restoration
and recovery.

Labeling addiction as a disease de-emphasizes the fact that men
and women who live independently of God in sinful rebellion desperately need the cross of Christ and can, in God's power, overcome sin. In
the attempt to make life "work" apart from God, more and more professionals are defining aberrant behavior in disease terminology rather
than facing the consequences of the Fall. This definition arrogantly pre-
sumes that we can reduce the complexity of human behavior and figure
out how to fix it.

According to the biblical model of sexual addiction, treatment of
the behavior alone can't ultimately resolve the difficult and complex
problem of sexual addiction because such behavior is caused by original sin. This model says that a devastating condition exists within the
hearts of all people that can't be cured merely by treatment focusing primarily on destructiveness and loss of control over sexual behaviors. The
biblical focus isn't on a disease that causes a problem but on humanity's
deceitful heart that continues to create far greater problems than sexual
dysfunction.

The most significant cause or source of sexual addiction, according to the biblical model, lies within each person. Paul said it well in

Romans 3:23—"All have sinned and fall short of the glory of God." Sin is an integral part of our nature. The Bible says that the heart is deceitfully wicked (Jeremiah 17:9, Hosea 10:2). It is an interminable maze of intricate motives and responses. Each of us has the tendency to act in our own self-interest. We search for experiences that increase positive outcomes and decrease negative ones. Instead of trusting God to meet our needs for safety, control, purpose, and meaning, we often trust ourselves and try to order our own lives.

In this life we may have wrenching distress, but we must recognize that God will overcome the world and its sinfulness. When Christ returns and all bow before Him, we will be fully restored, fully healed, and pain-free (Revelation 21:4). Meanwhile, we face challenge and pain, but also moments of great joy, in our flawed relationships in this imperfect world.

If we see sexual addiction through the lens of the medical disease model, we drift into the trap of calling any destructive behavior an incurable ailment rather than a sin requiring the power of Christ for deliverance.

A disease concept of sexual addiction eases the burden of guilt by ignoring the fact that sex addicts have made damaging choices to fulfill their own demands. At some point before their behavior seemed to fly out of control, they chose to use sexual fulfillment to compensate for the painful emptiness and loneliness of a fallen world. Eventually they reached a point where they strongly believed that sex was love and that they couldn't live without it.

Within the deep recesses of sexual fantasy with a perfect partner, sex addicts can create the illusion that what the soul craves can be provided with certainty. These individuals are highly motivated. They demand to control their needs, and in that demand create the illusion that they've found what they couldn't find any other way. Thus, to stop their sexual behavior seems like a death sentence.

This feeling of power over pain, hurt, and loneliness causes the sex addict to repeat whatever will create that feeling again. Desire leads to need. Desperation leads to actions that will meet the need. Because the satisfaction of that need is temporary, the action must be repeated and becomes a habit.

❖   ❖   ❖

Phil, a thirty-year-old youth pastor with three children, found himself frequently masturbating at the office and at home. On a youth retreat, he was drawn to a new girl in the group, Michelle. She was fourteen, vivacious, friendly, with long blonde hair and developing breasts. Being around her in the kitchen, during Bible studies, and in recreational times made Phil feel warm inside and alive. He was certain that she was attracted to him, too.

By the end of the first day, Phil was having detailed fantasies about Michelle. Lying in bed, he imagined her inviting him into the woods and seductively taking off her clothes. He was overpowered with desire as he thought about her maturing figure and the way she looked at him. He could almost hear her voice asking him to partake of sensual pleasure.

As he filled his mind with these passionate thoughts, he knew they were wrong but he could think of nothing else. Sleep seemed impossible, so when he heard a noise downstairs he decided to investigate. Finding nothing, he started up the stairs, knowing he'd pass the room in which Michelle and her two friends were sleeping. He imagined her in the hallway, suggesting to him that they go to the empty room at the end of the hall. By the time he reached her room, he couldn't help opening the door to look at her. He stood there, looking at her face covered by the soft moonlight. Feeling powerless, he walked into the room to get closer to her.

"Pastor Phil," one girl said, waking up, "what are you doing?"

Stunned, Phil clutched for an answer. "I thought I heard something." The girl, with innate trust in her youth pastor, returned to sleep. But Phil was shocked at the reality of what he had done. By noon the next day, however, he was again fantasizing about Michelle and found an excuse to return to his room to masturbate. He had become powerless to control his masturbation, fantasies, and now risky voyeurism.

Sinful behaviors do provide a certain level of fulfillment or they would never be tempting. They offer a momentary escape or the illusion of relief. But following our sinful desires always suppresses the truth of who God is and what He says about us in the Bible. When we don't allow God to be who He is in our thinking, when we choose to worship other things in His place, self-created things in life become our substitute gods. The central issue is idolatry. The truth about God is suppressed by our wickedness (Romans 1:18). As we honor God, we'll move to honor others. As we dishonor God, we dishonor ourselves and others.

Three times in the opening chapter of his letter to the Romans, Paul uses the expression, "God gave them over." When we don't honor God, God also responds. When we sin in our hearts toward Him, refusing to be dependent on Him, He gives us over to the control of the sinful things we prefer more than Himself. When God gives us over, He turns us over to the darkness of our hearts, which creates deeper darkness. He gives us over to our own cravings, allowing us to be controlled, literally, by those desires.

Therefore, moral perversion is the *result* of God's wrath, not the *reason* for it. God's action is severe in that He gives us over not only to our desires but to a condition of ungovernable desires. We demand; God steps back. We choose to regulate our lives rather than honoring and obeying God; we lose the ability to regulate our desires. In *The Problem of Pain*, C. S. Lewis states that people will "enjoy forever the horrible freedom they have demanded, and are therefore self-enslaved."[1]

Our sinful condition is terminal. We can't extricate ourselves from sin. We can't transform our sinful condition by determination, treatment, or willpower. We are "spiritually dead" without Christ. We don't just commit evil acts; we have a propensity to commit evil. Paul warned, "People will be lovers of themselves . . . abusive . . . without love . . . without self-control . . . lovers of pleasure rather than lovers of God" (2 Timothy 3:2-4).

Truly it is part of God's grace that sexual addiction cannot ever completely eliminate relational pain or bring lasting satisfaction. Thus sex addicts can be motivated to ask God to search their hearts and remove the suppression of truth so that they can see the true, sinful direction of their hearts.

When I counsel sex addicts, I help them identify their real, though often hidden, goals. Gradually they realize that their behaviors are indeed the result of unconscious choices. Instead of being out of control, trapped into committing an endless series of sexual acts, the addicts learn they can make different choices to achieve their goals. They can choose to trust God to help them respond honorably to the pain in their hearts and their desires for personal satisfaction, regardless of the confusion and disappointment life brings.

It's easy to see why many people find it easier to embrace the medical disease model than the biblical model. Obviously what people believe about human nature, creation, the existence of God, and other presuppositions are important decision factors. To people who believe that people are inherently good, sympathetically treating sexually addicted people with compassion seems more humane than holding them individually responsible for at least part of their choices and addictive behaviors. But we can't treat psychological issues the way a dentist fills a decayed tooth. We can't simply control behavior without dealing with the underlying issue of sin. Sexual addiction can be a metaphor for the human condition. We can treat sexually addictive behavior, but we can't heal the condition of the human heart.

Unless treatment programs address people's deceitfulness and rebellion of the heart, they can't deal with the fundamental issue underlying sexually addictive behaviors. To take any other position is to say, in essence, "Sin can be dealt with apart from what Christ did for us on the cross."

Let's look at several evidences of sin in the lives of sex addicts.

Arrogance and Pride
As addicts seek to create their own meaning in life, to produce a sensation of potency, and actively to challenge a hostile environment that brings overwhelming feelings of fear and helplessness, they become self-reliant. They depend on what they can do for themselves rather than on what God can do for and through them. They create patterns of behavior that allow them to maintain pleasurable states of being rather than admitting that they can't cope with their problems and turning to God and others for help. In short, they arrogantly believe they can solve their problems on their own, that they can nurture themselves, and that fulfillment in life can be self-created.

Unfortunately, when people seek a "taste of Heaven" by their own means they create a living hell of uncontrolled desires. By refusing to let go of their hope in themselves, sex addicts create a world in which they can neither truly satisfy themselves and avoid pain nor appreciate and trust in what God promises He will provide. They create a self-perpetuating hell of unremitting anguish that demands moments of illusory relief through more sexual behavior and the fantasy of being loved.

Selfish Demand to Have Needs Met Now

God doesn't promise to fulfill all our desires in this life. Only when we acknowledge our helplessness and our inability to meet our deepest needs can He pick us up, enable us to see ourselves as we really are, and provide eternal restoration and healing.

But sex addicts spurn the promises of God. They are compelled to use sexual behaviors to meet their needs on demand. Refusing to face relational emptiness, they deny or minimize the disappointments others have caused them. Or when they are disappointed, they seek relief and satisfaction through reliable sexual acts. "If I can't get what I want through my job," one pastor admitted, "a prostitute is just around the corner, offering me a different type of abundant life."

Yet sex on demand can never meet our deep internal needs. Loneliness, fear, anger, and other feelings creep back after each moment of false sexual intimacy. After a time, if the behaviors no longer satisfy the way they used to, greater demands must be met. Eventually sex addicts reach the terrifying conclusion that sexual intimacy can't relieve their deep, unmet longings. Thus even the experience of sexually addictive behavior creates resentment at the deepest levels of the human spirit because the individual can't satisfy all internal needs.

Fear of Pain

"Cast all your fears on me because I'll care for you," said God. But sex addicts allow paralyzing fear to motivate their behaviors. On the surface, they may cry out to God for deliverance from addictive destruction. Beneath the surface, however, their hearts don't call on God in desperate dependence. They choose reassuring, consuming, and predictable lives lived out in sexual addiction as a form of defensive withdrawal. In their hearts, they don't believe that other people, or even God, are interested in responding to the real void within them. They fear the risk of learning the truth. Escape is what's important. They lack faith in God's promises to stand by them in their struggle to know the intimacy and fulfillment only He will provide.

Thus sex addicts develop a contempt for genuinely intimate relationships. Full of self-contempt and rage at the prospect of never having their needs filled by others, sex addicts rely on behaviors that don't require another person's deep involvement. Sex becomes a form of self-preservation in a hostile world.

All sinful human beings naturally seek ways to protect themselves from pain and uncertainty. Sexual immorality is just one avenue many people try. But there are some unique factors—secondary to the deceitfulness of the human heart—that contribute to the development of sexual addiction. Let's examine them briefly.

SECONDARY FACTORS THAT CAUSE SEXUAL ADDICTION

Even at early ages, children develop ways to cope in order to protect themselves from painful circumstances. Following are some of the painful situations that cause children (and adults) to develop behavioral patterns that can lead to sexual addiction.

External Elements that Can Influence Sexual Addiction

Inconsistent parental nurturing and love. The family is the most important context in which children learn how to be intimate with other people. Physical touching, for example, is first experienced in the family. Ideally, feelings and thoughts can be freely expressed and affirmed within the family. But relationships, by nature, are disappointing. Lack of parental nurturing and acceptance can destroy children's natural desires for intimacy.

Inconsistent love and nurture make children suspicious of the "good times" with Mom and/or Dad. *I like being with my parents,* a child may think, *but at the same time I'm afraid because they can be so scary to me.* That child might look forward to going fishing with a parent while staying on guard for the sudden, unpredictable moment when the parent becomes angry because a fish gets away.

Children in such an environment feel powerless to get their parents to care about them or to stop the painful disappointment that tears at their deepest being. Feeling inadequate and unlovable, they may long for change and blindly hope that one day things will be different and they will be able to control their situations and relieve their feelings of loss of control, deception, and uncertainty. They may be driven to do whatever is necessary to give them a feeling of secure, consistent love. That desire may drive them into fantasy and false intimacy.

A sense of parental betrayal. When parents don't provide the emotional and spiritual support their children need and rightly desire, the children may feel betrayed. They may be unwilling to develop trust because trust seems to lead only to false hopes and more pain. They learn that intimacy within the parent/child relationship is not safe.

Children who are betrayed feel great loneliness, abandonment, and self-doubt. *Can I trust you in this relationship?* a child wonders. *Can I even trust how I feel? Perhaps I just shouldn't feel.* When the ground of relationships is perceived to be barren, it's easy to see why children view relational distance and false intimacy as alluring, safe, and justified.

Insufficient parental teaching and modeling. Every child needs a model of intimacy. Ideally, the best way for children to learn what intimacy is all about is through their experience with their parents. Parents need to model affection so that children can learn that kissing, holding hands, and hugging are expressions of how people feel about each other and that physical expression is normal and appreciated.

Of course the opposite is also true. In many homes, parents teach their children that sexuality is "dirty" and that emotional closeness is to be feared, not treasured. Instead of learning the value of intimacy, children learn that intimacy brings pain and that the best way to survive is to withdraw from others. They learn that sexuality is something to be criticized or abused. They don't see from their parents a biblical model of sexuality in which the male and female complement one another and use their gifts and abilities to share God's love with others. As a result, children are left to develop an understanding of relational intimacy that is all too often based on ignorance and false patterns of self-fulfillment.

Child abuse. Many sex addicts were victimized at young ages. Child abuse does far more damage to children than inconsistent love and nurture or insufficient parental teaching and modeling. Children who are physically, sexually, or emotionally abused learn early that love and expressions of affection are too often twisted to benefit others, that passion and desire are selfish and hurtful. Thus true intimacy—and even the desire for intimacy—is a fearful enemy, and children come to believe that it's important to protect themselves at any cost. When these children grow older, they may use fantasies or other people to provide pseudo-relationships that are safe from the intimacy that terrifies them.

Early sexualization. Sexuality doesn't begin at puberty or on a wedding night. It begins in the womb, a time of close physical intimacy. At birth the child's entry into the world can be a gentle experience of what it means to be nursed, cuddled, and nurtured. In some families, however, babies and young children are exposed to sexual sounds, smells, sights, or touches that are inappropriate. They may be exposed to actual sexual abuse, view pornographic pictures, see people having sexual relations, or hear people speak about sexuality in graphic terms.

Young children aren't emotionally prepared to deal with early sexualization. They lack the cognitive development to process sexualized thoughts and feelings and literally don't have a vocabulary. They can't control their exposure to or participation in sex, and thus can become innocent victims.

Early sexualization exploits young children's innocence and makes them feel insecure. As they get older, they retain these experiences in their subconscious minds and may make choices based on their early learning.

Stress. Many events cause stress in children's lives—too many, in fact, to list. The stresses that create such feelings as helplessness, abandonment, and despair add to other external factors and may drive children to find relief through false intimacy. Many sex addicts have told me that they engage in their behaviors of choice to relieve stress or to reward themselves for coping so well during stressful times.

Internal Elements that Can Influence Sexual Addiction

In addition to what's happening in children's lives externally, a number of internal changes are taking place. Children are learning how to respond to others, how to cope with relational difficulties, and how to process new thoughts and powerful emotions. The following factors can, individually or collectively, influence children toward sexually addictive behavior.

Emotional numbness. Events and emotions press in on children from every side. How they respond depends on whether they view each event as good or bad. It's a fact that there's something disturbing about everything, even things that are good. The wagon is fun to play with, but it may break. The new friend loves to do fun activities but suddenly decides to befriend someone else. The toys need to be picked up. Good friends move away.

Some children, when faced with relational pain, have the ability to go on and risk again with other people. They continue to hope and, despite the negatives, to feel positively about life and what it has to offer. Other children become emotionally numb, unwilling to risk, seeking to control the amount of pleasure and pain in their lives. Children who learn to bury their emotions deep inside—who deny their true feelings—are candidates for sexual addiction because false intimacy brings sensations, activity, and excitement that counter their paralyzed inner feelings. If a child grows up believing that true intimacy isn't possible, that fulfillment in life isn't attainable, and that emotions are to be feared, that child may choose false intimacy.

A controlling self-orientation. All of us, philosophers or not, think about who we are and what we need to do to achieve happiness in life. Sometimes children who are wounded by life's realities come to believe that they can actually find fulfillment, or at least improve life, by self-determination—by what they do. They don't want to be dependent on God or trust others.

This approach to life may work quite well for a while. When a child experiences rejection, for example, he or she can take steps to relieve the pain—perhaps by withdrawing. Insulating oneself from pain can lead to a certain type of security and peace.

The problem occurs when, in creating an illusory world in which they try to control what happens, children miss the true dynamics of life—the rewarding relationships that may sometimes be painful and the excitement and rewards of taking risks. And of course children, like adults, can't create true fulfillment on their own. It's not possible to solve every problem or at least make it better. Not every person can be manipulated into loving another.

The bottom line is that every person is helpless. Only God can bring lasting peace and joy. When people learn to act independently of others and God, they become self-indulgent. They develop strategies that they perceive will help them achieve personal satisfaction and meet their own needs.

SUMMARY

Whenever we look at the cause of something negative, it's essential that we become aware of *why* things don't work. That may seem like a simple statement, but in reality it requires a profound understanding of what life is really about.

The popular way to understand what life is all about is to look at the human condition as defined by our own understanding rather than by God's wisdom communicated through the Bible. Without God, we look at what's wrong with us and conclude that it's connected to what others have done to us—the environment in which we grew up, the society in which we live, our economic conditions, and so on. So we conclude that if we change the economic conditions or the level of functioning within our families and avoid being victims, we will change what is causing us to do negative things or what is causing others to do negative things to us.

On the other hand, when we start our evaluation of life with an understanding of God and recognize that the deeper causes of our problems are rooted in sin, we begin to have a different awareness of why things don't work, why there are problems, why people become addicted. We can more appropriately understand what is required to truly make positive changes, to make a lasting difference.

The origin of what is today called sexual addiction lies in the human heart's stubborn determination to obtain what only God in His grace can provide. It is foolish to exhort sex addicts to stop their behavior. Addicts become powerless over their behavior not because it's a disease but because God has responded to the arrogance of the human heart by turning people over to the control of their evil desires. Addicts' powerlessness over their sexual behavior doesn't even compare to their impotence to change the fabric of their sinful heart. Only Christ can grant them true freedom.

John Stott said it well:

> If we bring God down to our level and raise ourselves to his,
> then of course we see no need for a radical salvation, let alone
> for a radical atonement to secure it. When, on the other hand,
> we have glimpsed the blinding glory of the holiness of God and
> have been so convicted of our sin by the Holy Spirit that we
> tremble before God and acknowledge what we are, namely
> "hell-deserving sinners," then and only then does the necessity
> of the cross appear so obvious that we are astonished we never
> saw it before.[2]

None of us can be God. He is the Creator; we are the creation, profoundly dependent on Him. God desires that we will face the emptiness of our fallen relationships. He wants us to recognize our inability to gain lasting satisfaction from relationships alone and our inability to protect ourselves from pain.

Life in this fallen world is intolerable. We can rail against God, others, and ourselves. We can choose to indulge in false intimacy. We can seek to bury our pain through sexual addiction or many other addictive or nonaddictive behaviors. Or we can patiently wait for the day when there will be no pain and realize that God is building each of us "to become a dwelling in which God lives by his Spirit" (Ephesians 2:22).

CHAPTER
✦ 4 ✦

Hope for Those Who Are Sexually Addicted

B y all appearances, Joe was a successful pastor. His church was growing. He had two fine sons and a wife who took pride in her family and was consistently involved in church and community activities.

But things weren't as perfect as they appeared to be. When he was arrested for soliciting a prostitute, Joe's sexual addiction made front-page news. His sons were ashamed to show their faces at school. His wife, enraged, felt betrayed and went into a deep depression. His church forced him to resign in public disgrace.

During the next two years, Joe came to me for counseling. Like many sex addicts I've worked with, Joe's restoration didn't begin until others discovered his addictive behaviors. For years he had vowed that he'd get help for himself, but he never had. Only when he had no alternative was he willing and able to deal with his problems and receive help. Together we worked through his years of addictive behavior, the trauma of "being caught," the shame he had brought on himself and his family, his eventual divorce, and his struggle to enter a new career.

During one of his appointments, he walked into my office, grinned, and said, "I'm a free man!" And he truly was. He was finally free from the bondage of prostitution, pornography, fantasizing, masturbation, and extramarital affairs. He could look freely into the eyes of his family and friends. He felt free to worship the Lord with genuine delight and passion, and felt with deep sorrow and grief the wounds and losses that went back to his childhood. He laughed and cried as he began to taste the joy of his restoration with God.

Perhaps you identify with Joe because you're involved in addictive sexual behaviors. No one else may know about your addiction. Others close to you may know but be unsure how to respond to you. Perhaps your addiction is harming other people. Whatever your situation, *there's hope.* There are ways in which you can receive compassionate help and deal with the issues that have made you afraid of true intimacy. Your relationship with God and with others can be renewed.

If much in this book describes you, I urge you to continue reading. Joe is one of many former sex addicts who has learned the meaning of godly sorrow rather than worldly sorrow and has gained a peace and a joy that pass understanding. There is more to life than the fevered pursuit to relieve pain and taste the pleasures of false intimacy for a season.

FACE YOURSELF HONESTLY WITHOUT DENIAL

Denial is a common way by which people avoid facing the trauma of emotional upheavals and dealing with tough issues. Denial acts as a buffer between who people would like to be and who they really are.

Many sex addicts, for example, deny the reality of God and His laws. They deny that they are created in His image and that He is the Creator. They love false gods — the god of others' opinions, the god of personal image, the god of self-gratification. They try to create their own realities and deny the seriousness of their addiction.

But ultimately, none of us can avoid the anguish of the soul that longs for relief from fear and relational pain, that longs to admit the fantasy of the illusions, and that longs to replace the shame of self-centeredness with the God-given strengths of love, vulnerability, and selflessness.

If you are a sex addict, you'll remain trapped in addiction until you stop denying your addiction or thinking that it's not serious enough to worry about. You'll be unable to escape the shame and guilt you feel — and possibly suffer even worse consequences than Joe did. Denying or minimizing sexually addictive behavior and its effect on other people paralyzes the restoration process.

Denial is a strong enemy. It works hard to construct a false world that is perceived to be safer than the one God created. If you use sexual behaviors to feel safe or to create a sense of intimacy (that is really anything but intimate), you are taking what is true about God and suppressing it by your sinfulness.

❖   ❖   ❖

Before he was released by his law firm, Larry, a lawyer and sex addict, had several affairs with women whom he determined were weak, vulnerable, and hungry for relationships.

Later, while participating in group therapy, Larry had to listen to women describe the deep damage they had experienced when men had used them sexually. "As I listened to those women," he said to me, "I wilted inside. I realized that I had used rationalizations to justify my behavior toward women like them. I had used the fact that my wife was cold and sexually uninterested as a way of justifying my use of other people."

Larry's small opening to the truth of who he was allowed God's light to penetrate even deeper parts of his soul. The wretchedness of his heart was more nauseating and the sorrow more grievous than he had imagined, but later the joy of being dazzled by the grace of the loving God was much richer than he could have imagined.

❖   ❖   ❖

To quit denying that you've been using others isn't easy, as Walt discovered: "For years I've felt ashamed of the filthy thoughts I've had when I'm around women. If they knew my thoughts, they'd literally run away in fear. The thought that I could think such things is absurd, but I'm that monster. The heart that fueled such thoughts is worthy of even stronger repulsion, but when I think about being forgiven, it's incredible!"

Rick, crying convulsively, recalled molesting a younger girl in a barn when he was nine. Bill, an accountant, nearly vomited as, for the first time, he admitted fondling his eight-year-old sister when he was sixteen. As he faced what he had done, he buried his head in his coat.

Shame causes us to hide, to cover our faces. But in some cases it opens the door to the deepest, most disturbing shame when we realize we have arrogantly shut God away in the closets of our lives.

Imagine a teenager who, in his father's absence, rejects his mother's curfew and locks her into a closet before leaving home. As he ends his late evening, which has been full of fun and games, and returns home, he knows he must face not only his mother but eventually his father, who will return in several days. He knows that his actions have been reprehensible and that the consequences will be severe.

Imagine this teen's surprise when, as his mother comes out of the closet, she firmly backs him against the wall, rebukes the hideousness of his disrespect, and then embraces him, exclaiming with tears of joy how thankful she is that he is safe and home at last.

This is an unbelievable story, but it illustrates the surprise of the gospel and the Lord's response to us when we allow Him to have free rein of our lives. The son in our story will remember the excitement of a wild evening with friends, but the warmth of his mother's eyes despite the horror of his offense will probably stir him to honor her as never before. Likewise, legitimate shame over the ways we've violated our relationship with God allows us to experience the jolting shock of His love and to change our direction so that, with eager hearts, we want to warm the heart of another.

Allowing yourself to face your secrets and what you've done will be frightening. You'll have to deal with anger and fear. Recognizing the ways in which you mentally, emotionally, and/or physically violated other people will make you feel ashamed. But you, like every other sex addict, must face the ugly truth of what is in your heart and admit to more than your addiction in order to start down the road toward change and healing.

RECOGNIZE YOUR NEED TO CHANGE
Simple recognition of addictive behavior is not on its own enough to accomplish healing. Sex addicts who stop living in denial and recognize that they have hurt others and turned away from God may not always have an urgent desire to change. Their tears of sorrow over their addictive behaviors may spring more from the fear of being rejected and feeling ridiculous than from genuine brokenness and repentance.

In order to begin the process of renewal, you must choose to stop hiding from yourself—from the depth of your feelings, from the pain, from others. You must choose to turn away from your lack of dependence on God. You must stop trying to protect yourself by dealing with sexual addiction on your own. You must refuse to believe that you can control situations that provide you with what you need to make it through each day. In short, you must face the truth that the shining, untarnished image you offer to others is a heinous attempt to deny your sin and your need of God's mercy and grace.

That's tough to swallow, isn't it?

One of the finest resources in the list of recommended reading at the end of this book is *Inside Out* by Dr. Larry Crabb, which deals in great detail with issues of internal change. (See appendix A, page 195.) Dr. Crabb, too, concludes that the first level of internal change takes place when you decide to change your direction. You realize that you have sinned and must turn to Christ and live for Him.

Next you must face the intent of your heart, which will always be to move away from God, to rebel rather than honor God as God, to find some way to manage your pain and disappointment on your own without turning yourself over to your Creator. As you face your natural self, you'll feel grief and sorrow that your persistent attempts to make life work on your own have led you astray from true intimacy with Him.

FACE YOUR WOUNDEDNESS

If you're like other sex addicts I know and care deeply about, you're wounded inside. One patient described the loneliness he felt at age four when his father died. He longed for a male figure to play with, fish with, or simply be with. So when an uncle invited him to go fishing and said to be ready at 5:00 a.m., the boy was delighted. But 5:00 a.m. came and went. The uncle never showed up. "That incident," he told me, "combined with others, caused me to insulate myself from the world of intimacy. I don't want to trust anyone's offer of relationship again."

It may be that you're a victim of physical, sexual, or emotional abuse. Perhaps the pain you feel concerning relationships is nearly too heavy to bear. Maybe your spouse has been cruel to you. Possibly you were neglected as a child and lacked assurance that you were nurtured or protected. Maybe your parents seldom or never told you that they loved you. Maybe your father or mother was too busy to make time for you.

Perhaps disappointing relationships have left you confused about intimacy. You wanted to enjoy the pleasure of being emotionally and/ or physically close to someone, but your history has proven that relationships bring hurt and are therefore dangerous. So you used false intimacy that felt like closeness, that provided physical and emotional relief, and that gave you a sense of control over your life. You felt justified in your control of relationships and your pursuit of what was best for you, regardless of what it cost others.

The real issue isn't how deeply you were wounded, but what you've done to protect yourself from further wounds by turning to false intimacy. The issue is also whether or not you'll allow your woundedness to prevent you from loving God and others.

If you choose to stop protecting yourself, the reality of your sin will be more terrifying than you can imagine. God's hatred of sin is like a "consuming fire." If love is deep and true, it will never deny the stench of sin. God has no place for pretense. If His love is to have any meaning, any life-changing power, it must expose what is true about you and me.

As a sex addict, the thought of facing even more shame and the truth of what you deserve will seem intolerable. God's love, which is unique and illogical to the natural mind, is often met with confusion and resistance. Yet the journey of renewal is like no other path.

Before you can move toward God, you must fully acknowledge how deeply you desire relationships with others and how deeply you've been disappointed. This doesn't have to move you toward anger against God. Instead, it can move you toward hunger to know Him more.

Dr. Crabb says, in addressing what he terms the second level of internal change, that we must change our approach to relationships. We must recognize the deep hurt and disappointments that we've experienced and agree that our primary commitment to avoid pain and achieve some level of personal satisfaction is wrong. Our devotion to self-protection and control might be very human and natural, but it is the essence of sin and will keep us from ever loving or being loved.

REALIZE THAT YOU CAN'T HEAL YOURSELF, AND TURN TO GOD

Walls of prideful independence reinforced with rods of anger don't easily fall down. The issue that will begin knocking the walls down is whether you are truly motivated to seek genuine, lasting change instead of settling for a simple remedy.

Do you passionately want to know God and His will for your life?

Are you willing to be constrained by His law of love in order to know what it means to receive His healing?

Do you believe that God truly loves you and has your best interests at heart?

Do you truly believe that you can't provide yourself with the kind of fulfilling life you long for?

Can you recognize your sinful desire to seek an abundant life on your own?

Can you admit your feelings that God has abandoned you and that it's your right to find relief and do whatever is necessary to provide for and protect yourself?

If you can answer yes to these questions, then you're on the way to healing and restoration.

Receiving restorative healing is much more than simply renewing your own efforts to do what's right. It's much more than just choosing to stop your addictive behaviors. Without God's help, you can modify your behaviors through willpower, perhaps even stopping them for a long period of time. But you'll continue to wrestle with internal struggles with no hope of conquering them. Sin is too strong to overcome on your own. You must pursue God on His terms, in brokenness and humility, facing the sinful condition of your heart and inviting God to begin healing you.

The Apostle Paul wrote in Romans 6:18-23 to Christians who have had to deal with tough issues:

> You have been set free from sin and have become slaves to righteousness. I put this in human terms because you are weak in your natural selves. Just as you used to offer the parts of your body in slavery to impurity and to ever-increasing wickedness, so now offer them in slavery to righteousness leading to holiness. When you were slaves to sin, you were free from the control of righteousness. What benefit did you reap at that time from the things you are now ashamed of? Those things result in death! But now that you have been set free from sin and have become slaves to God, the benefit you reap

leads to holiness, and the result is eternal life. For the wages
of sin is death, but the gift of God is eternal life in Christ Jesus
our Lord.

Paul later added, "Therefore, there is now no condemnation for those
who are in Christ Jesus, because through Christ Jesus the law of the
Spirit of life set me free from the law of sin and death" (Romans
8:1-2).

TRUST GOD TO SATISFY YOUR NEEDS

Although I grew up in Christian circles, I became confused for a time
about what it meant to trust God. The concept of trusting God was not
only elusive, but empty.

Since then I've met others who felt the same way. When someone
says, "Trust God!" we know this truth is supposed to be meaningful to
us, but often it stirs little movement within our beings. Clichés about
trusting God have sometimes left us angry and wondering if it is even
possible.

Perhaps the concept of trusting God can feel so empty because the
person urging us to do so knows little of the reality of trusting God in
his or her own life. Perhaps trusting God feels empty because of our
own lack of spiritual maturity.

What does it really mean to trust God with our lives? Which desires
of our heart will be satisfied?

As you evaluate your life and deal with its inevitable disappointments, it's easy to begin feeling as if life is a threat. It's easy to assume
that God's function is to offset that threat and improve your life. It's
easy to assume that trusting Him means to believe that He will do
this. Yet nothing could be further from the truth. A quick reflection on
the first-century church reveals that New Testament Christians never
attempted to validate the truth of Christianity by the way in which their
experiences in life improved. For them, becoming Christians meant real
sacrifice and sometimes death.

Frequently, trusting God with our lives goes no further than
desiring a change in circumstances or relationships. We direct our
desires at God, expecting Him to come through with what we want
so that life will be worth living. We "trust" Him so that He will
make a positive difference in how things are going. Personally, I've

often felt that if I trusted God in a difficult circumstance my agony would decrease and I'd glide through the difficulty as if on a magic carpet. *After all,* I'd think, *isn't God supposed to make a difference in my life?*

In *Mere Christianity*, C. S. Lewis wrote, "If I find myself having a desire which no evidence in this world can satisfy, the most probable explanation is that I was made for another world."[1] All of us have unsatisfied desires, but which desires can we trust God to satisfy? He has promised to satisfy the deepest desires of our hearts, which are ultimately the desire to know and be intimately connected to Him. The psalmist expressed this desire when he wrote in Psalm 42:1, "As the deer pants for streams of water, so my soul pants for you, O God."

Perhaps few of us have the courage to sail far away from familiar shores and pant after God. Paul's words about hardship unnerve me as I imagine talking with this weathered man. "We were under great pressure," he says, "far beyond our ability to endure, so that we despaired even of life."

I'm tempted to observe, "Aren't you being a bit dramatic? How could it be that a man of your spiritual stature could ever be reduced to trembling?"

Paul adds, "Indeed, in our hearts we felt the sentence of death."

"Wait a minute, Paul," I break in, troubled. "Why would anything so overwhelming happen to a faithful servant of the Lord?"

With a look of patient strength in his eyes, Paul gently says, "This happened that we might not rely on ourselves but on God, who raises the dead" (2 Corinthians 1:8-9).

If these words pierce my heart, perhaps I can begin to address my arrogance and lack of dependence on God. Perhaps then I can begin to discover what it means to trust God.

While I was in private practice in New York City, a young woman called to request an immediate appointment. I had an opening and saw her that same week. She arrived at my office in tears and impatiently waited for the appointment to begin. Then she announced, "My husband returned from work earlier this week and said he was leaving to live with his secretary, with whom he'd been having an affair. I begged him to stay. I pleaded with him to consider our children and to have concern for our life together. But he packed and quickly left. What am I going to do? I can't live without him." As the counseling session ended, she said she felt encouraged and set up another meeting.

At the next session, she came to my office smiling. Before she even sat down, she declared, "Everything is all right!" Suspecting that her husband had not returned, I was surprised. Then she said, "I realized that God doesn't support adultery and that He wants our relationship to be restored. It's God's will for my husband not to live in sin and to return. Obviously this will happen. I just need to have faith that God will do it. I do have the faith, so it'll happen. I feel fine now. Thanks for your help. Further counseling won't be necessary."

I felt extremely uncomfortable as she described her trust in God. As I questioned the wisdom of her approach and her biblical basis for trusting God in this way, she became offended. "God is a good God," she insisted. "He won't let me be alone. He will bring my husband back. I know He will. He will honor my faith!" Since further conversation seemed pointless, we ended the session.

Like many of us, this woman believed that difficult situations place an obligation on God to respond according to what we define as necessary to our well-being. So our trust in God often stops short at expecting a change in circumstances. We don't develop a deep faith and trust in His character. We assume that the fig tree must grow and provide fruit if God is good and if we are to rejoice. Our trust is in what we insist God will *do* for us. Surely He eventually will come through and meet our needs in this life.

Once, during a counseling session, I challenged a young, unemployed man, "What if you don't get a job?" Repeatedly he answered that eventually he would find a job and that God would meet his needs. I persisted in asking the same question and then added, "Would God be good if you went another six months . . . a year . . . two years without a job?" The harder I pushed, the more uncomfortable he became.

Similarly, many of us often present our petitions to God in ways that almost obligate God. Describing the problem of a demanding spirit, Dr. Larry Crabb stated, "To trust God means to demand nothing."[2]

As I learn to trust God, I acknowledge how little I really know of what it means to rely on God and demand nothing. I've seen only a glimpse of what it means to put my confidence in God in a way that goes beyond a demand for safety and comfort. Yes, I have tasted what it means to have faith in God with deep contentment and a strong resilience that is not easily deterred, but I've only begun to trust.

Scripture tell us that we can trust God in the midst of any relationship. However, a determined decision to move toward such trust is a decision to enter the reality of a fallen world that is at best disturbing. If we want to trust God and know His loving power, we have to face much about ourselves that will be disturbing beyond imagination.

When we become responsive to the Holy Spirit, nothing will be more unsettling than our violations of love. We've been self-centered rather than other-centered. Sexually addictive behaviors are not as dark as the internal commitment to serve self that results in even the most subtle violation of love. Real spiritual and relational change requires a commitment to move far beyond the certainty of false intimacy toward unsettling and sometimes shattering levels of disappointment that we reach when we really love others. Only then will trusting God become more than a sermonic platitude. Only then will it become the rock on which we stand.

ACKNOWLEDGE YOUR NEED OF REPENTANCE

The process of dealing with sexual addiction is a process of repentance. For some, the word *repentance* conjures up images of preachers pounding on pulpits, demanding that we get right with God and flee our sins. Consequently, it can seem more like an act of shaming than a challenge to move toward God. Yet repentance essentially means *to change direction*. It means to turn *away* from a focus on yourself and your own autonomy and *toward* God.

When you come to God with a sense of desperation, trembling in your heart because you realize that if He doesn't respond and meet your needs you can't receive ultimate fulfillment, you're ready for the deeper work of God's Spirit. Thus repentance is a critical step in the process of experiencing deep internal change.

The real question isn't, Are you sexually addicted? The real question is, Are you living your life by demanding that you fulfill your desires and avoid all pain? You must go far beyond the head knowledge that admits you are simply "passing through" this world toward the eternal home you've never seen. Sexually addictive behaviors can seem boring when you are truly captivated by God's purposes.

This point becomes clearer when we contrast the love of self-denial with the "love" of sexual fantasy. A sexual fantasy stems from a desire to gain more in a relationship than is possible. It's an attempt to gorge ourselves with passion and move into a state free of any chance for disappointment. Simply put, we want to enter the Garden of Eden again.

But the very desire to know the bliss of the Garden here on earth is skewed by our obsession with self. In demanding the bliss of someone's real or imagined warmth, we become consumed with ourselves, which destroys the very ecstasy we seek. There is no way out. We are locked in reality, always wanting and therefore always destroying what we want. The process is insane. Until we become consumed with the love that desires to give for the sake of another's good, all joy is an illusion.

One sex addict began to realize this when he understood that his pornography and masturbation were direct results of his fear of loving his wife. "It is safer," he said, "to masturbate and look at a magazine. What you want me to do is impractical. I'd rather be with a caged lion than attempt to love her."

Many of the illusions we design to find fulfillment are sexual. We believe that if only someone attractive will touch us with warmth, everything will be okay. God wants to strip us of our illusions. We receive a clear picture of this in the book of Hosea, where God describes our relationship with him as "adulterous" whenever we attempt to find satisfaction in resources other than Him.

Hosea's relationship with the adulterous Gomer symbolizes God's message to an adulterous generation. God orders Hosea to bring back his philandering wife and keep her isolated for a while (Hosea 3). This isolation conveys the idea that Gomer is deprived of the sexual relations that previously gave her an illusion of fulfillment. "You are," Hosea says, "to live with [wait for] me many days; you must not be a prostitute or be intimate with any man, and I will live with [wait for] you" (Hosea 3:3).

By this action, the false intimacy of Gomer's promiscuous life was stripped away. The isolation unveiled her pain. She had no ability to cover her agony by gorging herself on the warmth of a man's sensual touch. The effect of isolation is striking, unnerving, and consistent with the God who demands nothing less than total devotion. The effect of God's actions causes people to come trembling to Him (Hosea 3:5).

False intimacy deludes us into believing that we can enjoy passionate warmth in fantasy, in a phone call, or in the arms of a prostitute. God, however, wants to deprive us of anything that is meaningless or counterfeit. He wants us to experience isolation when we need it, to be pushed to the point of discovering that we can't fulfill ourselves, to face the reality that life in this world will never be fully fulfilling: Emptiness and disappointment are chronic realities.

We naturally (and wrongly) kick and scream when we are forced to face this reality. We may even accuse God of negligence and mis-management by protesting, "If only I hadn't been sexually abused," or "If only You had given me a warmer wife." When we justify and rationalize addictive behavior, we temporarily escape the isolation and inadequacies of a fallen world. Until we face the reality of our situation, godliness seems extremely impractical and the foolishness of false inti-macy seems more than reasonable. Without repentance from a trem-bling heart, self-denial is absurd. As one sex addict put it, "Stopping the sexual addiction was easy. Loving even those who have or would harm me—now that's impossible! Such love would have seemed like committing suicide, but I know that deep within me, God is calling for me to follow such love."

Repentance must include a sense of God's high calling to love and a sense of humility. Each time a sexual temptation comes—and they will—boldly ask yourself in openness and honesty, *What is this doing for me? How does it protect me? How deeply does it satisfy me? In what ways have I failed to love?* Allow yourself to sorrow over the damage you have caused to yourself, to your relationship with God, and to others.

Repentance is not simply a decision or an act of your will to stop addictive behavior. It's not just a new effort you make. Rather, *it's an act of God and His grace that occurs as you open yourself to God and the deep work of His Spirit in your heart.* Through repentance, you begin to understand that you aren't in control of discovering the source of true fulfillment or protecting yourself from pain. You begin to be disillu-sioned with the directions you've been heading in. You begin to thirst for real spiritual change.

CONFESS YOUR SINS BEFORE GOD

Once you acknowledge your helplessness and dependence on God, real change can occur. Then you can take the next step and confess your sins to God.

Imagine yourself looking courageously into God's eyes, which aren't vengeful, bored, or patronizing. Refuse to defend yourself or to justify your behaviors because of what others have done to you or because your deepest needs have remained unmet. Face the gravity of your sinful heart.

After David committed adultery with Bathsheba, he turned to God and wrote,

> Wash away all my iniquity
> > and cleanse me from my sin.
> For I know my transgressions,
> > and my sin is always before me.
> Against you, you only, have I sinned
> > and done what is evil in your sight,
> so that you are proved right when you speak
> > and justified when you judge.
> Surely I was sinful at birth,
> > sinful from the time my mother conceived me.
> > > (Psalm 51:2-5)

Like David, you can admit that you have failed to love God, that you have run from Him and others into your own illusion. Search your heart before Him for the pervasive unmet needs that, above all else, pushed you into the horrors of your double life. Acknowledge before Him in a simple prayer that you are helpless, weak, and frail. Confess your sins before the Lord, who promised in 1 John 1:9—"If we confess our sins, he is faithful and just and will forgive us our sins and purify us from all unrighteousness." Remember that Christ "gave himself for us to redeem us from all wickedness and to purify for himself a people that are his very own, eager to do what is good" (Titus 2:14).

When you pray and confess your sin, know that God is listening. James wrote, "Therefore confess your sins to each other and pray for each other so that you may be healed" (James 5:16). God knows your heart and can transform your mind. He alone can cleanse you of your sin and remove horrible memories.

If you have never asked God to come into your life, invite Him in. He promises to respond to your invitation. "Here I am," He says. "I stand at the door and knock. If anyone hears my voice and opens the door, I will come in and eat with him, and he with me" (Revelation 3:20). Paul writes, "If you confess with your mouth, 'Jesus is Lord,' and believe in your heart that God raised him from the dead, you will be saved. For it is with your heart that you believe and are justified, and it is with your mouth that you confess and are saved" (Romans 10:9-10).

Jesus came to earth to take away your sins. He died a painful death on a cross but received new life again after three days.[3] If you just invited Christ into your life, or if you're just returning to Him after trying to live life on your own, believe that He has heard your prayer and will answer.

As you feel a growing, perhaps frustrating and scary, desire for true intimacy and are tempted to numb the pain again with addictive behaviors, God will help you resist the temptations. In James 4:7 you will find this assurance: "Submit yourselves, then, to God. Resist the devil, and he will flee from you." God will help you build new spiritual foundations and strengthen your growing refusal to revert back to the emptiness of false intimacy. As you get to know Him better, God will prove Himself trustworthy and begin teaching you His truths through the Bible, prayer, and the teaching of godly men and women. You'll begin to realize that the dreadfulness of the sinful human heart is more hideous than any of your sexual behaviors.

Through brokenness, hopelessness, and dependence on God, you will receive joy in your heart — your deepest desires and inner being — as you begin to pursue God. You will partake of what He alone can offer and move into real intimacy as you love others.

When you experience confusion and disappointment and you are convicted of the ways in which you fail to love others courageously, continue to give of yourself. Gradually your faith will develop. At times it will be weak, yet you will develop perseverance, endurance, and other character qualities.

As the Cross and the promise of Christ's Second Coming become more real to you, relational disappointment can give way to hope. In recent years I've come to feel a stirring in my heart, a sense of excitement, when I read Bible verses about hope. Paul, for instance, writes of endurance that is "inspired by hope" (1 Thessalonians 1:3). Spiritual hope is never directed toward what is tangible. It is an alluring hunger for what exists only in our Father's presence. "But hope that is seen,"

Paul writes, "is no hope at all. Who hopes for what he already has? But if we hope for what we do not yet have, we wait for it patiently" (Romans 8:24-25).

ASK FOR HELP

If you're willing to face your wounds and your sins, the next step toward healing is to ask for help. There are many reasons why you might choose to receive help. You may recognize that your addiction has produced tremendous pain in your life and in the lives of others. You may want to live in a less insane world, free of the haunting guilt and the bizarre double life you have been living. You may want to improve relationships with your family and friends. You may be worried about contracting a disease. Perhaps your bank account is drained by paying for 900 calls.

Often sex addicts begin to seek help because their circumstances are out of control and they feel overwhelmed. This motivation, however, is not sufficient to carry them through the mire of deep change. But it's a place to begin. Later, the hope of knowing the Lord more intimately will initiate lasting change.

When you acknowledge that disappointments exist in every relationship, you will be drawn to seek fulfillment in Christ alone. Whatever your reasons for seeking help, however, don't wait, as many sex addicts do, until relationships with people close to you are disrupted or destroyed, your reputation is shattered, your career is on the line, you are being interviewed by a policeman, or your finances are in a shambles.

One man who telephoned me for help said, "I just realized that my addiction could cause my death. After years of pornography, making 900 calls, and masturbation, I just had anonymous sex in the rest room of a bus stop."

Listen to the small voice deep inside you that is urging you not to wait any longer, that is hoping secretly that someone strong will discover your addiction and confront you so that the insanity can end. Recognize the madness of what you are doing. You can be freed from the guilt of living in sexual excess. But sexual addiction involves complex issues, and it's important that you don't try to deal with them on your own.

God has given you three primary resources for help: the Word of

God, the Spirit of God, and the people of God. These three interlocking elements are essential to your restoration.

The Word of God
God's Word penetrates more deeply than mere knowledge. It's as penetrating as the sharpest surgeon's scalpel, exposing the deadly cancer hidden in our hearts. Such exposure can lead to searing conviction and radical, lasting change.

If you read the Scriptures and are eager to be convicted of your sin, the Spirit of God will faithfully reveal what needs to be addressed in your life.

The Spirit of God
The Spirit of God is the primary resource for searching our hearts, for identifying the sin within us. Remember, all of us on earth are dealing with the problem of sin, which is much more severe in its consequences than sexual addiction alone:

> The heart is deceitful above all things
> > and *beyond cure*.
> Who can understand it?
> "I the LORD search the heart
> > and examine the mind,
> to reward a man according to his conduct,
> > according to what his deeds deserve."
> > > (Jeremiah 17:9-10, emphasis added)

Our cry must echo the psalmist's: "Search me, O God, and know my heart; test me and know my anxious thoughts. See if there is any offensive way in me, and lead me in the way everlasting" (Psalm 139:23-24). Listen to your prayers and the prayers of others. A prayer like David's is rare, isn't it? Why do people neglect the discipline reflected in this prayer? Perhaps just the thought of such an inner examination makes us feel uncomfortable or even fills us with terror. People frequently pray to know God's will and ask Him to provide for their well-being, but rarely do they invite Him to take a penetrating look at their hearts and point out how they fail to follow His will.

We must not take the Holy Spirit or His work lightly, either by ignoring Him or by assuming that He will do a shallow, ineffectual job if we invite Him to examine our hearts.

The People of God

One great concern I have is that few people of God can be effective resources for you, a sex addict. The Body of Christ should be a great resource, but with immense sadness I admit that the Church is often unwilling to grapple with the sin, deceit, and behavioral problems that exist in people's lives.

Nothing disturbs me more than Christians who falsely assume they are doing well spiritually, who assume they are close to being perfect. I believe such arrogance is a stench in God's nostrils.

Without hesitation or fear, the writer of Hebrews warns and directs us, "See to it, brothers, that none of you has a sinful, unbelieving heart that turns away from the living God. But encourage one another *daily* . . . so that none of you may be hardened by sin's deceitfulness" (Hebrews 3:12-13, emphasis added). Having warned the readers of Hebrews about the problems the Israelites faced in the wilderness, the writer cautions them not to commit a similar sin—implying that the same problem could occur again. In this context, the writer urges the readers to mutually encourage each other, rather than to live in isolation.

Christian fellowship is the relational context in which people's hearts can be softened and the damage of deceitfulness avoided. The exercise of love should penetrate so deeply that it lessens the possibility of people becoming hardened.

Regrettably, too few Christian counselors really know how to deal with problems of sexual addiction. If you're beginning to feel a real need to reach out and work on your problems, finding a Christian counselor may be difficult. The best way to locate one is to talk in general terms with others, including Christian friends and pastors, to find out who they recommend. Perhaps you will find a competent Christian counselor who doesn't know much about sexual addiction. During your first session, find out if he or she is willing to read this book and other resources in order to become more familiar with the dynamics of sexual addiction.

If a Christian counselor isn't available in your area, don't lose heart. Seek out a trustworthy Christian friend or a godly pastor who is willing to learn about sexual addiction, who will encourage you to deal with key issues, who will keep your confidence, and who may be able to link you up with another person who can provide the professional counseling and understanding you require.

PURSUE HEALTHY RELATIONSHIPS

As God begins working in your life, you can begin to love others as God created you to do.[4] Under your counselor's guidance, move toward others courageously. Don't deny the pain of disappointments in relationships. Face them squarely. Allow yourself to hunger for deeper relationships, and as you draw closer to God be assured that He will draw closer to you. He will give you hope.

RECEIVE A PHYSICAL EXAMINATION

If your addiction has involved sex with another person (other than your spouse, if you're married), you need to have a gynecological or urological examination in order to detect sexually transmitted diseases (STDs).

Chlamydia, for example, can cause inflammation of the urethra in men and pelvic inflammation in women. Without medical treatment, it can lead to infertility or can give unborn babies eye, ear, and lung infections. In some men and women, chlamydia has no apparent symptoms but can be transmitted to a sexual partner.

Gonorrhea and syphilis, two better-known STDs, can cause serious problems if they aren't detected early. Gonorrhea can cause sterility and pelvic inflammatory disease in women. Both can infect babies during birth. Syphilis can cause brain damage in men and women and can also weaken the heart and blood vessels.

AIDS, the most deadly of the STDs, has no cure and eventually results in death. At the in-patient treatment program where I've worked, each sex addict who has had sexual contact with another person outside of marriage is given an HIV test because in its early stages AIDS has no symptoms. As the disease progresses, AIDS patients exhibit symptoms of secondary infections because their immune systems break down.

Herpes also has no cure. It is life-threatening to unborn babies, can cause blindness if it spreads to the eye, and has been linked to cervical cancer in women.

Genital warts, a virus, also has no known cure and has reached epidemic levels in the United States. Usually a urological or gynecological examination is necessary to diagnose genital warts.

CONSIDER JOINING A SELF-HELP GROUP
Three different organizations address the issues of sexual addiction: Sexaholics Anonymous (SA); Sex Addicts Anonymous (SAA); and Sex and Love Addicts Anonymous (SLAA). Self-help groups started through these organizations exist throughout the United States. Although the organizations themselves are not Christian, quite often Christians attend local meetings. To find the address of the group nearest you, check your local telephone directory or call the National Association for Sex Addiction Problems: (800)622-9494.

Usually, attendees at a self-help meeting exchange telephone numbers and relate on a first-name-only basis. In most groups there are sponsors available to help you who are more experienced in the treatment of sexual addiction and have worked through issues of sexual addiction themselves.

The advantages of attending local meetings with other sex addicts include finding personal support, gaining more information, and having help and encouragement in working through a crisis. You'll be in contact with people who have problems similar or even identical to yours and who are also tempted to revert back to prior behavioral patterns.

At this point allow me to share a strong caution. These self-help groups primarily focus on a twelve-step model of recovery. Many thousands of people have benefited from twelve-step programs. However, as you know from reading the previous chapters in this book, much of the medical-disease model of addiction on which these programs are founded fails to address the deep issue of sin in the heart. Therefore, if you become involved in a recovery group, I encourage you to pray that the Spirit of God will search your heart and help you address issues that might be neglected in a recovery plan.

In *The Voyage of the Dawn Treader*, C. S. Lewis provides a wonderful description of change on a level much deeper than we ourselves can accomplish. Eustace, a main character, describes to his cousin Edmund how he changed from a dragon back to a boy with the help of Aslan the lion. First, Eustace tried desperately to peel off his scaly dragon skin, but each time more scales reappeared. Finally Aslan said, "You have to let me undress you." The process of being changed wasn't inviting. Eustace described it this way:

> The very first tear he made was so deep that I thought it had gone right into my heart. And when he began pulling the skin off, it hurt worse than anything I've ever felt. The only thing that made me able to bear it was just the pleasure of feeling the stuff peel off. . . . Well, he peeled the beastly stuff right off—just as I thought I'd done it myself the other three times, only they hadn't hurt—and there it was lying on the grass: only ever so much thicker, and darker, and more knobbly looking than the others had been.[5]

If the heart isn't cured, taking a series of steps toward behavioral change will ultimately accomplish little.

CHANGE IS A PROCESS

Welcoming the coming of true change in your inner being involves recognizing that it will be a lifelong process. Radical restoration will take you on a journey that will do much more than simply reduce your pain and salve the wounds of sexual addiction. It will go beyond causing legitimate and positive changes in your out-of-control behaviors and reducing the consequences of your behaviors. God is able and willing to redirect your deepest thoughts and emotions throughout your lifetime, to guide you toward new ways of responding to people and situations, and to heal you from the inside out.

Your healing will never be complete, since we all live in a sinful world. But in Heaven, everything will be as it should be: "He will wipe every tear from their eyes. There will be no more death or mourning or crying or pain, for the old order of things has passed away" (Revelation 21:4). The end result of your process here on earth will be reflected in your eternal life to come.

Meanwhile, prepare yourself for some bumps and bruises. When you reach for deeper levels of relational change and long to receive healing and forgiveness for past and current wounds, there's a real possibility that you'll receive new wounds. People can be cruel, judgmental, and unwilling to forgive. But with God's help and the help of others, you'll have the resources to deal with these wounds. (Appendix B, page 197, lists ministry resources you can consult for help.) Change is possible, but not without pain that may stir your desire to return to the temporary protection of false intimacy.

I'm writing these words on my twenty-third wedding anniversary. I'm fortunate and deeply grateful for Rosemary, who offers me a lasting, inviting love. In many ways that thrill my heart, she is easy to love. But both of us would quickly confess that we are very unlovable, too. I admit that when she seems unlovable, withdrawing from her, if only to pout, is an inviting option that could even appear to be justifiable. As I mature spiritually, however, I hear the whisper of the Spirit of God saying, "Even now you must love her." With sorrow I admit that I can and sometimes do harden my heart toward her. I choose the safety of a book, a television program, or—most commonly—my work. Sin is subtle. Dealing with it through God's power requires courage. But when I confront my sinful desire to avoid relationship, I feel joyous and peaceful, not just because Rosemary responds to my openness, but because I experience the delight of knowing God more deeply.

Dr. Larry Crabb addresses this in what he calls the third level of change, which requires change in the direction of our being. This direction is reflected in Psalm 73:25—"Whom have I in heaven but you? And earth has nothing I desire besides you." Said another way, in this life we must recognize that we will inevitably experience disappointments, pain, and a lack of complete relational satisfaction. When we stop fighting this reality and become willing to accept it, we can be free to move into the world with a real sense of purpose and direction. Like Jesus, we can become committed people who will deny and sacrifice ourselves in order to love others.

Accepting reality doesn't mean we stop longing for a better day. As Paul said, all of us groan as we strive to live and love in a fallen world:

> We know that the whole creation has been groaning as in the pains of childbirth right up to the present time. Not only so, but we ourselves, who have the firstfruits of the Spirit, groan inwardly as we wait eagerly for our adoption as sons, the redemption of our bodies. For in this hope we were saved. (Romans 8:22-24)

Meanwhile we groan, longing to be clothed with our heavenly dwelling, because when we are clothed, we will not be found naked. (2 Corinthians 5:2-3)

Life as we experience it now isn't what we want it to be. Rather than becoming paralyzed with disappointment and anger, however, we must realize that there's much more to come in Heaven. There, God will provide us with what we really desire, what we've been created to experience. Meanwhile, we groan.

Groaning essentially allows us to look at life as it really is, to understand that we can't easily provide what we long for and need, that we can't always protect ourselves from pain and disappointment. We desire to be in perfect relationship with God and others, to be free of hurt and pain, but none of this will happen in this life on a level that will completely satisfy us. So we have to groan and wait, looking with hope toward that day when all tears will be wiped away. In that hope, we will not be disappointed.

CHAPTER

❖ 5 ❖

Responding to Your
Sexually Addicted Spouse

T he evening had gotten off to a great start. Terri's husband had returned from work early, the kids were excited about spring break, and the whole family seemed to be in a relaxed, festive mood.

But for Terri, the happiness was short-lived. While hunting for stationery, she found homosexual pornography under the bed. She crumpled into the bedroom chair, her eyes filling with tears.

Should I say something to him right now? Terri wondered. *I might just say all the wrong things. And I'm scared of how he might respond. What should I do? Who can help him?* Then she chastised herself. *Maybe I'm jumping to conclusions — how could I have such horrible suspicions about him? What's wrong with me? How could I doubt him?*

Many people lived with their spouse's sexual addiction for years without knowing it. Others live with the pain of knowing but don't know how to respond. In order to remain married, they become numb to their feelings, or they just "turn the situation over to God," believing that prayer and "trusting God to take care of it" are enough. Still others, like Terri, suddenly recognize symptoms, begin to put the pieces together, and know that the addiction may require treatment.

If we discover that our spouse has a sexual addiction, the news is devastating, no matter how we find out. The blow will leave us feeling dreadfully alone—as if no one else in the world has ever married a sex addict—and possibly feeling incapable of sharing what's happening with anyone else. The great sense of loss can make all our dreams of "living happily ever after" vanish into thin air. We can't trust our spouse any longer; there's no security left in the relationship. We may question our own masculinity or femininity. It feels as if we're drowning, going down for the last time and powerless to do anything about it. Grief is overwhelming, for the marital relationship that once existed has been lost forever. Life will never be the same.

On learning that her husband had been having multiple affairs, a woman said to me, "I feel like my guts have been ripped open and are lying exposed to everyone."

A WORD OF ENCOURAGEMENT

If your spouse is sexually addicted, you're not alone. Husbands and wives across the country know firsthand what it's like to live with a sexually addicted spouse. You're not imagining things. You're not crazy. Your suspicions and dread are not unfounded.

Perhaps your spouse has communicated that his or her sexual addiction is your fault, that you were doing something wrong or that there's something lacking in you. Perhaps your spouse said something like this: "You gained weight" . . . "You're getting old and don't turn me on any more" . . . "I need more sex than you give me" . . . "If you satisfied me more, I wouldn't need to do this" . . . "This is just the kind of person I am and you need to accept that" . . . "I have some unusual sex needs and I don't think you're willing to fill them" . . . etc. Such rationalizations enable the sex addict to deal with his or her own guilt and shame, but unfairly place a heavy burden on you. Perhaps, attempting to save your marriage and cope with your spouse's behaviors, you accepted such rationalizations.

Perhaps you've become involved in sexually addictive behaviors yourself because you felt that you had no alternative and believed that doing them would help your spouse and your marriage. Maybe you've visited a topless or male striptease bar with your spouse or have had sex with multiple partners. Maybe you've watched raunchy pornographic films with your spouse, who hoped that this would improve the level of sexual intensity in your marriage. Maybe you've had sex with someone while your spouse watched. Perhaps you've even become sexually addicted as a result of being exposed to or participating in behaviors at the insistence of your spouse.

If so, perhaps you wonder what right you have to try to confront the problem. You feel shame and disgust, since you have "stooped so low." Maybe you even think there's no way out.

Regardless of your situation and how much the sexually addictive behaviors have progressed, *there's hope for both you and your spouse.* I encourage you to believe that sexual addiction must be addressed and to be willing to take the risks needed to deal with it. The place to start is in your relationship with God.

A WORD OF CAUTION

If you are married to a sex addict, I realize that this chapter may irritate you. Chances are, you've bought this book to find hope, some answers and direction, and some guidance on what to do or how to restore your marriage. I will offer you guidelines, but I can't promise you that your marriage will be restored. I can't promise that your spouse will stop sexually addictive behaviors. The best that I can offer is to help you move closer to God.

One wife said to me as she became aware of her husband's affairs, "Give me my life back! Take me back to twenty minutes before we started talking; I want my husband back just as he was!" Her plea wasn't so much an outburst at me as it was a statement of desperation as the black cloud of sexual addiction engulfed her life. She wanted to return to the safety of the world she had known before sexual addiction entered her home.

When hurting spouses come to me, my goal isn't just to restore their marriages and "give them their lives back." My goal is also to help them make a necessary shift in their hearts and perceive that only God is the source of true fulfillment. He alone can overcome the sin in our hearts that damages our relationships.

If you're a spouse of a sex addict, my heart hurts with you even though I don't know you. I know your hurt and your desire to regain your dreams. So many times I've sat with couples whose lives have been devastated by sexual addiction. I feel deeply honored by God to have this opportunity to minister. But a part of me hates my job. Why? I hate watching the agony of spouses who are married to sex addicts when they learn about the addiction. In many ways I'd rather inform them of a spouse's death.

What I have to offer won't provide a new path to a restored marriage or, for that matter, a salve for your deep wounds. More than anything, I want you to consider your relationship with God as you deal with your spouse's sexual addiction. Does a voice deep inside you whisper, "God is still good," even though you're married to a sex addict? If not, or if you fear that the whisper will soon be silenced, I have a message for you.

HOW YOU RELATE TO OTHERS AND TO GOD

The most difficult questions for a spouse to face in the nightmare of sexual addiction are: "What has been going on with me?" "Who am I?" "What am I about?" "What makes me the kind of spouse I am?" As we tackle these questions, we begin to understand the deepest purposes of our hearts. Solomon wrote, "The purposes of a man's heart are deep waters" (Proverbs 20:5). Since it's rare for most of us to contemplate how we relate to others, most of our purposes are hidden deep inside.

Yet it's important for us to delve into our heart's purposes. We need to ask when and how we have been hurt in past relationships. We need to ask if, because of that hurt, disappointment, and damage, we have made a subtle and seemingly reasonable commitment to avoid being hurt. As we lift the shield of protection around us, do we feel energized and stronger? Deep inside, can we make the following statement? *I may not get the love I want, but I'm stronger as I avoid the pain.*

The best shield of protection is contempt, either for ourselves or others. If we pour contempt on ourselves, we feel less desire to be intimately involved with others. *How could anyone want to spend time with me?* we reason. While painful in and of itself, this thought functions as a diversion for the greater pain of not knowing how to make relationships work.

Contempt directed toward others keeps them away. *Don't ever come near me again, you jerk,* we may think. But beneath that thought is a subtle attempt to protect ourselves as we try to control painful disappointments in relationships. In effect, we provide our own explanation of why relationships hurt. Contempt is like wearing a stiff brace; it hinders our movements but protects us from further injury.

Both types of contempt exist in a marriage, often in a subtle form.

"I learned a long time ago, even with a full-time job, not to expect him to help me around the house or with the kids," a woman might say. "That way, it never bothers me. You're fortunate, but new husbands are that way. Just wait. Your husband will change in time, too."

In this all-too-common interchange, the wife honestly wants help — or, on a deeper level, she wants the sense that her husband cares enough to desire to be helpful. The fact that she sees him as never helping is a mild form of contempt, because she chooses to view him as showing less concern for her than he could. Through her assessment of him, she eases her pain of disappointment.

Imagine a friend who says to you, "If I had gone to college or was just smarter, I know Bill would talk with me more." Here the contempt for self blocks the intensity of the loneliness a spouse feels when she's left out of conversations. She avoids the issue by directing the pain inward. If she were to ask honestly why her spouse avoids serious conversation with her it would be like wading toward the deep end of a pool without knowing how to swim. Taking refuge in self-contempt is a strategy to ward off the danger of further hurt.

Facing past hurts is never easy. We simply don't want to acknowledge that life often disappoints us. With few exceptions, patients who describe the pain in their relationships with their parents frequently add a qualification, such as, "Well, my dad (or mom) did have a rough childhood." If I comment on the severity of their abuse, they respond by saying something like, "But I think my dad really did care in his own way." To face our past wounds is to know the horrifying reality that we were powerless to prevent the damage that happened to us or to produce the love we so deeply desired.

To face the current and inevitable disappointment that exists in our marriages can feel like dropping into a deep well, the depth of which we can only imagine fearfully. To taste what we desire and don't have is to know the level of helplessness that either moves us toward God or drives us toward insanity. If we listen carefully, we can hear the unsteady beat of our deceitful hearts in our stubborn commitment to stand on our own in finding fulfillment and avoiding pain.

I'll always remember the experience of sitting in a cave, in what seemed like hundreds of feet below the ground. Having turned off the light on my helmet, I experienced true darkness for the first time. I felt my eyes refusing to accept the complete lack of light as they struggled desperately to focus on something. I remember the eerie feeling of putting my hand directly in front of my face and not seeing it. It wasn't an inviting experience. I believe the depth of my heart is such a scary place.

Yet if we dare, we can seek out the real issues at the core of our hearts. Most of us will discover that when we relate to others, even to a spouse we have promised to love and cherish, we do so with self-centeredness or self-protection. We don't want to face the fact that we've failed to love our spouse in significant ways. That feels as if we're beginning to crawl on our bellies into a dark cave. So we tend to believe in our own goodness. We believe that our commitment to be good will prevent our marriages from eroding and omit the possibility of heartache. "He's the one who had the affair. I've been faithful all these years."

❖   ❖   ❖

June, a pastor's wife, had been married twenty years when she discovered that her husband had been having affairs in every church they pastored. "I thought that if I committed my life to Christ and His service," she sobbed, "and married in His will, problems like this would never happen." Like many of us, she depended on herself and her own goodness to ensure a strong marriage, obtain happiness, and avoid disaster.

As we talked together, June found it difficult to release the illusion that she was good and that she could make life "work." She never claimed to be a perfect wife, but she needed to take a penetrating and difficult look at how she had failed to love. Denial comes so easily; integrity, the willingness to humbly accept who we really are and how we relate in self-centered ways, comes only after great struggle.

"I've been such a fool," June said later. "I was trying to do and be good in order to make my life happy. I lived for myself and called it godly living." She began to acknowledge not only the extent of her husband's sin, but her own failure to love and how it had affected her marriage. She then was able to desire changes in herself, not just in her husband or their marriage.

June also realized that she didn't want to change merely to get her husband to stop his sexual activities. When she looked deeply into her heart, she knew that making the change was both necessary and impossible to do on her own. At this point God became a necessity in her life — a Savior, not just an enabler — and she desired to know Him in a way she'd never known before.

❖   ❖   ❖

What are the parallels to your life? As in June's case, you're not responsible for your spouse's addiction. Nevertheless, you are responsible for the kind of spouse you have been. Have you always been devoted to your spouse, willing to do whatever it takes to make him or her comfortable but unwilling to confront tough issues? Have you avoided conflict with your spouse at all costs and never intruded on his or her time? Have you made sure you never said no to making love, even though you no longer cared much about it? Have you been angry, lonely, and feeling inadequate?

Answers to questions such as these can point out areas in your life where change may be needed. Perhaps you are very dependent on your spouse and a bit distant. You can't function without your spouse. Decisions scare you. Perhaps you haven't become relationally involved with your spouse and have kept others away with your temper. When people tried to get close, you didn't trust them.

Whatever your style of relating, it probably seems to work for you. But beneath the pretenses, you've made a commitment that you will never be hurt again if you can help it. This commitment conflicts with the commitment to love. Being vulnerable isn't easy, especially when you've been offended and victimized by your spouse.

As you face your spouse's sexual addiction, it's much harder to avoid the relational pain of living in this fallen world. Resist the temptation to try to put all the pieces back together. Examine your heart under the floodlights of God's Spirit and the piercing love of a counselor or true friend. You need someone who will challenge you to shift your focus from the problems of sexual addiction to who you are now as a wife or husband and who you need to become.

As you examine yourself and your motives, you'll head in one of two directions. Either you will harden yourself to shore up your own defenses while you try to rely even more on yourself, or you will soften, allowing your self-reliance to seep away as you know God more intimately. This latter process will be painful, but it is only through the fire of such self-examination that any of us can be refined.

IT'S IMPORTANT TO DEAL WITH YOUR SPOUSE'S SEXUALLY ADDICTIVE BEHAVIOR

If the process of examining yourself and your relationship with God is so challenging, why even deal with the sexual addiction? *Because you can't allow yourself to die inside.* You don't have to live life singing in a minor key. You can be free to sing a new song and leave the living hell that sexual addiction creates. You can be a part of the restoration process that brings healing and hope to you, your spouse, and others you love. You can gain insights into yourself and grow closer to the Lord as you rely on Him for strength. If you deny your spouse's problem or try to ignore its seriousness, you will do great damage to yourself and possibly allow others to continue to be hurt.

Obviously there's no guarantee that your spouse will be willing to receive treatment and be restored. But your willingness to try your best and work toward restoration with your spouse is an important part of your own spiritual growth and emotional healing. Whether or not your spouse agrees to receive treatment, at least you can experience restoration, healing, and a deeper passion for God.

In addition, God calls us as Christians to love one another, to weep for others, to long that others will experience the abundant life that Jesus proclaimed. We are also called to pursue holiness, to stand firm against sin. Sometimes that means confronting those we love. Dealing with your spouse's sexual addiction will require great courage. There's a lot at stake when you lovingly intervene on your spouse's behalf.

With the help of a counselor, the prayers of faithful friends, and God's work in both your lives, positive changes may take place in your spouse, too. If you have the courage and commitment to deal honestly and courageously with what is going on in your marriage, you both may experience a new level of intimacy with each other and with God.

SOME BASIC ASSUMPTIONS

Before we go further, I'd like to detail a few assumptions to place the remaining part of this chapter in perspective. I'm assuming the following.

1. There are significant indicators that your spouse is involved in sexually addictive behaviors, which are affecting his or her life and possibly the lives of others.

The goal of this section is not to help you prove or disprove the existence of sexual addiction, nor to encourage you to go on a "witch hunt" to uncover evidence of sexual addiction. For instance, if a husband and wife are sexually uninterested in one another, that might be a symptom of a spouse's sexually addictive behavior. But it may also be due to other reasons, such as a medical problem or fatigue from grueling work schedules. Uncovering sexual addiction and using certain evidence to try to prove or disprove whether sexual addiction exists is an extremely complicated process that's beyond the limits of this book.

If you suspect that your spouse is sexually addicted, it may be helpful if you go back to chapter 2 and review the various types of sexually addictive behaviors. Indicators of sexual addiction may include: child pornography; learning that your spouse has had multiple but impersonal affairs or is having a purely sexual, non-emotional relationship with one person; expensive 900 number calls on phone bills; discovering sexual fetishes; finding out that your spouse is peeping in other people's windows; symptoms of child abuse in your children; and your spouse's involvement in prostitution.

2. Although the behavior of each sexually addicted person can generally be identified in one or more categories, it must be evaluated in light of many complex issues. Therefore, I won't describe how to deal with each individual type of sexually addictive behavior. There are simply too many varied and difficult situations for me to address them all accurately. Only after familiarity with your situation can a counselor recommend the steps you should take to deal with your spouse's specific addictive behaviors.

3. My third assumption is that you—the spouse of a sexually addicted person—are willing to address your spouse's problem, help your spouse receive professional help, and work toward restoring your relationship. I won't encourage you to use your spouse's sexual behaviors as an excuse to be irresponsible at home and not fulfill the needs of the family, or as an excuse to leave your marriage if it can be saved.

4. All the guidelines in this chapter are designed with two goals in mind: to help you receive the support you need, including encourage-

ment to obtain counseling; and to help you encourage your spouse to enter counseling.

In marriages involving the sexual addiction of a spouse, many relational issues need to be addressed. Vital relational issues may have been denied and ignored for years. Sexual addiction, sometimes a symptom of how far the marriage relationship has deteriorated, forces people to focus attention on problems that need to be addressed.

Even if the sexual addiction problem appears to be minor, it may be affecting you, your family, and the quality of your relationship with your spouse. As the sexual addiction continues, it may progress to deeper levels and become increasingly more difficult for your spouse to conceal. It's unlikely that he or she will be able to lead a double life for an extended period of time, particularly when the behaviors involve other people and may have serious financial, health-related, legal, or career consequences.

FACING THE REALITY THAT YOUR SPOUSE IS SEXUALLY ADDICTED

When you first learn that your spouse is sexually addicted, your emotions may conflict with each other in a volatile competition. Let's look at some of the common responses experienced by spouses of sex addicts.

Initial Denial

Sexual addiction and a healthy marital relationship are not appropriate housemates. The problems of sexual addiction must be addressed, although it will be extremely difficult to admit that they exist.

Part of the way people protect themselves from the intense pain of relational disappointment is to avoid looking honestly at their relationships. To maintain peace and happiness and avoid further hurt, it's tempting to deny what's going on.

When you look at the relational problems that exist in your marriage, your illusions will shatter. You'll have to face the reality that you haven't been willing to face honestly. The world appears safer when you try to push that reality away by clinging to reactions such as, "I can't believe this is happening" or "God wouldn't allow this to happen." But when you're unwilling to face what's going on, you're in denial. Real hope doesn't have a chance.

God calls all of us to look honestly at what life is really like. To do so only increases our hunger for Him if we understand that the earthly foundation we're tempted to build our lives on is not the true source of fulfillment. So when you begin to look at the problems of sexual addiction in your marriage, you will also be required to look at how you've constructed life to make it more satisfying. You will probably need to make changes in how you relate to your spouse.

It will be difficult for you to conclude that your world is unraveling. You may feel as if there is nothing left, that you have nowhere to turn. To move forward and grapple with sexual addiction means that your life will be thrown into chaos. Only God is a strong enough rock on which to stand.

Blame: An Element of Denial

Susan, a homemaker in the Midwest, was busy raising two young children while attending college part time. Frank, her husband, was often gone on business trips.

One day, when Frank had been out of town for several weeks, Susan decided that she'd better pay the phone bill instead of waiting for him to pay it as he usually did. When she opened the phone company envelope, she was startled to see that they owed more than three hundred dollars.

That seemed like a lot of money, since most of their family and friends lived nearby and they seldom made long-distance calls. So she looked over the numbers carefully and noticed quite a few 900 numbers. She called one of them, and someone began offering to talk with her in sexually explicit detail.

Shocked, Susan hung up the phone and called the telephone company. "This isn't our phone bill," she complained angrily. "It has to be somebody else's." The person at the telephone company checked the records and insisted that the bill was correct and that those numbers had been called. Susan could no longer deny what her husband had been doing.

When someone has clear evidence that his or her spouse has a sexual addiction, it's common to blame and focus anger on other people involved—or even on an institution such as the telephone company! In effect, this uses others as scapegoats in order to cope with the personal hurt and sense of betrayal.

Blindness to Symptoms

Ignoring symptoms of sexual addiction is another byproduct of denial. The spouse of the sex addict becomes aware of obvious symptoms—a library of pornographic films, photographs of prostitutes, child molestation—yet denies that these circumstances are indicators of something seriously wrong. A variation on this denial is when the spouse focuses on one issue, such as pornographic magazines under the bed, while denying that more major problems exist—even if he or she has been forced to engage in distasteful sexual practices. Essentially, the spouse is desperate to save the relationship and believes it's more appropriate to submit to the addicted spouse's demands than to take other action.

Inability to Accept the Seriousness of the Situation

Still other spouses notice the symptoms but think the problems will go away by themselves or be removed by God's intervention. Instead of taking action, they wait far too long for their spouses to stop addictive behaviors on their own.

Sometimes a spouse will talk with a number of friends until one of them agrees that "the problem really isn't that serious." Instead of taking steps that will lead the sex addict toward treatment and restoration, the spouse may develop tolerance to the behavior(s) or simply refuse to recognize its impact. Other spouses who recognize the symptoms simply "turn the situation over to God," believing that God alone will solve the problem without any action on their part.

Sometimes initial denial, like Susan's, leads to the inability to accept all the facts. It's understandable that a spouse may not grasp the seriousness of sexual addiction quickly. When I have cautioned spouses of sex addicts that complete healing will take a long time, they commonly say to me during the first few weeks of counseling, "I'm glad that my [husband/wife] is doing so well. [He/she] hasn't behaved addictively and obviously is committed to change. I think [he/she] has turned around."

Sometimes a spouse wrongly assumes that shame will motivate a sex addict to stop repulsive behavior once it has been discovered. A woman I know is married to a man who had a homosexual lover for a number of years. When she discovered that relationship and told her husband what she knew, she assumed that he'd stop his homosexual behavior. She thought that his behavior was so abnormal and unnatural that he'd stop as soon as it was exposed. She didn't realize the extent to which her husband had been living a highly secretive, double life and that the rejection and shame of others weren't strong enough to influence his actions. For ten months her husband stopped cruising gay bars and being sexually involved with other men. Then he experienced a crisis in his job and began cruising again.

Feelings of Sexual Inadequacy
It's common for a man who discovers that his wife is sexually addicted to discount or even deny the problem. In general, a man gains a great deal of identity and security in his masculinity through sexual relations with his wife. So when he feels that he can't establish and maintain a meaningful sexual relationship with her and sexually satisfy her, he feels deeply inadequate and wants to deny that the problem exists.

It is equally true that the wife of a sex addict feels unattractive and sexually inadequate. *If I'd been thinner, more attractive, more sexy,* she may think, *my husband wouldn't have this problem.*

Denial enables people to avoid difficult facts and can therefore ease the pain. But using denial as a means of coping with a spouse's sexually addictive behaviors leads only to further pain. The addicted spouse needs help. Most likely he or she can't stop the behavior or even control it. Many sex addicts whose spouses know about their sexual addictions continue to progress to even deeper levels of addiction. Hope can develop only as a result of extensive counseling with a spiritually mature helper who is competent to address the complexities of sexual addiction.

Not long ago a woman shared her story with me. It illustrates why an objective counselor, not a spouse, is important in helping a sex addict work through deep issues.

> For several months after I discovered my husband's sexual
> addictions—his frequent affairs with prostitutes, his visits to
> porno shops and topless bars, the thousands of dollars of por-
> nography that he had amassed—I tried to be totally accepting
> and loving, looking at myself. I begged him to get help for
> his sake, for the sake of the kids, so that he could be in right
> relationship with God. I told him how much I wanted to work

through and understand the problem. But he only disappeared more. His excuses increased. And when I confronted him again about the reality of what he was doing to me and our family and to God, he said, "Your understanding and forgiveness make me feel more guilty," but he refused to get help.

DEALING WITH YOUR FEELINGS ABOUT YOUR SPOUSE'S ADDICTION
Feelings of Fear
It's common to feel paralyzing fear when it becomes clear that the sexual addiction must be addressed.

"How will my spouse respond to me if I get involved in this problem?" a woman asked me. "My whole life will disintegrate, and I won't survive. So much might happen if I work toward getting this resolved. I don't want to do anything, and yet I do."

It's hard to be objective and evaluate the price of doing nothing. What price will be paid if the sexually addictive behavior continues? What will happen to your ability to feel, to know God in a deeper way, and to share God with others? Who else could be harmed? You may feel it's safer to believe the lie that things will get better on their own rather than face an uncertain future.

The most important issue, however, is not what will happen *if* the sexual addiction is addressed, but what is happening *right now*—spiritually, emotionally, physically—to you, your spouse, and possibly your children. A little more of your feminine or masculine soul dies each day as you choose to live with sexual addiction.

Because you're afraid, you can choose to numb yourself, to "be strong" for the sake of your children. You may try to reason with your spouse and bargain with God. You may feel that only God can get you out of the addictive mess, but at the same time you may be frustrated, confused, and resentful that He allowed you to be placed in this situation.

Feelings of Anger
Once you accept the reality of your spouse's addictive behavior, you may go through an eruption of anger. In extreme cases, a normally calm and patient spouse may become almost suicidal or homicidal, seeking to die or to hurt (or even end the life of) the sex addict or some-

one with whom the addict has been sexually involved. You may hear words coming out of your mouth that you didn't even think were part of your vocabulary.

You will feel deep anger because it is so hard to believe that someone who has exchanged marriage vows with you and declared his or her love for you would have so little regard for you—your emotions, your health, your family. "How is it possible," women have said to me in various ways, "that a man who had such a good reputation as a husband and father could so easily have lied to me and my children? My world has been turned upside down. How can the man I married be such a hypocrite? He has been a pastor by day and solicited prostitutes at night."

Anger reflects your deeper hurt. It is justified, given your spouse's betrayal and the acts that he or she has committed. Learning that the spouse you have made love to has been having sex with prostitutes or is bisexual, for example, is a perfectly valid reason to become angry. There's also the anger that your addicted spouse has caused your life to fall apart. You may even be angry at God: "He allowed me to marry someone who has this problem. I prayed and really wanted His will. Why did He allow this to happen?"

This deep anger can be difficult to handle, especially if you're a Christian. Perhaps you believe it's wrong to feel anger, and you try to keep its raging torrents buried deep inside. That isn't healthy. Deep-rooted anger can lead to sickness and many other problems. It's important for you to choose to deal with your anger constructively. One of the best ways to do this is to talk with an objective third person—your pastor, a counselor, a special friend—who will keep your confidence and be a good listener.

Feelings of Betrayal

"How could he do this to me?" one woman yelled at me during a counseling session. "This fulfills my worst fears. Why did he do that with those other women? I've been living with someone I don't really know at all. I never could have imagined this would happen. I trusted him! I told him once that if he ever had an affair, I didn't think I could go on."

Betrayal is part of the deep hurt you feel. It's essential that you acknowledge this hurt and disappointment. Perhaps your spouse fantasized about other people while in bed with you. Perhaps your spouse has broken the marriage vows and had sexual relations with another person or many people, of the opposite sex or the same sex. In any case, it's clear that from now on life can't be what it was; the ideal image of your life is shattered. Your hope, which has been built on life being at least manageable if not wonderful, is gone. As a result, you must deal with the fact that you don't even know the person you married. Your spouse has carried on a deceitful double life, radically different from the life you have known and probably grown to love. Now you wonder if you'll ever be able to trust your spouse—or anyone close to you—again.

You feel that you've placed everything you had as a person into a fragile vessel and given it only to the person you married. You trusted that this person would see the beauty and delicate nature of that vessel, value it, guard it, and cherish it. You've given this person your most precious possession. But now you discover that this lover-turned-stranger has inventoried everything in the vessel and determined that it wasn't enough. What pain you now feel!

Feelings of Loss of Permanence

"I feel like my spouse has died," one woman said. "It hurts so much. Everything will change now, won't it? Nothing from now on will ever be the same." She understood that sexual addiction, particularly more serious types of intrusive addictive behaviors, change a couple's life forever. The couple can't go back to what life was like before. Their world is unraveling, and authorities—social services department, lawyers, police—may be involved, too. Sexually addictive behavior may drastically alter or even destroy reputations, careers, and families.

Although life after addiction is never the same, it won't necessarily be worse. As we'll see, positive changes can result when a husband and wife work together to deal with sexual addiction. Deep, positive change can take place in their overall relationship and their relationship with God.

Feelings of Withdrawal and Depression

It may be the case that you simply can't face the mountain of pain and the day-to-day challenges of dealing with a sexually addicted spouse. Hope seems too distant. Understandably, you withdraw, trying to insulate yourself from the struggle and the pain.

Extreme, long-term withdrawal, however, will damage both you and your spouse. It increases marital strains and may actually encourage your spouse to use more sexually addictive behaviors to gain false intimacy.

At this time, your addicted spouse especially needs your support and love, even if he or she is hostile and doesn't want to address the real problems. It's vital that you realize how important a role you can play in helping both of you recover from the effects of sexual addiction. It's important that you take action to make a strong commitment to face the struggles head-on. If you find yourself unable to cope and experience severe symptoms of withdrawal or depression, talk with a professional counselor, a pastor, or someone who understands why you feel the way you do and will help you work through it.

Feelings Regarding Sexual Intimacy
The quality of the sexual relationship in a marriage is usually severely affected when one spouse is sexually addicted. In fact, real intimacy between you may not have existed for years.

However, coping with what appears to be lack of sexual interest is quite different from coping with the fact that a spouse uses sexually addictive behaviors as substitutes for genuine expressions of intimacy. It's as if you've been living with a beloved stranger.

Spouses of sex addicts often believe that they can control their partners' sexual behavior. They act out this belief through their own sexual behavior, which is a defense against their helplessness and an attempt to protect themselves from more pain and disappointment. For example, the wife of a sex addict may dress seductively, buy sexy nightgowns or underwear, and participate in sexual activities that are distasteful to her or immoral. Other spouses may respond quite differently. As their marital relationships deteriorate in the absence of real intimacy, they may feel like sex objects and avoid or discontinue sexual relations.

You can't control the type of person your spouse is going to become or the quality of your marital relationship, but you can control the ways in which you relate to your spouse. As part of how you were created, God gave you the desire to be sexually intimate with the marriage partner you love, but having sex with your spouse now isn't worth the price of contracting a sexually transmitted disease. If your spouse has had sexual relations with any other people, you must make the decision to stop having sexual relations. Additionally, both of you should be tested for STDs.

In the midst of all the uncertainty you're feeling you may actually want to continue to be involved sexually with your spouse, even if you know that sexual relations with other partners is a past or present reality. You may be fearful that if you deny your spouse sex, you will drive him or her further into the arms of a prostitute or lover.

Please realize, however, that you are placing yourself at risk of acquiring a sexually transmitted disease in order to secure some sign of "love" from your spouse. Having sex will not prevent your spouse from continuing to look for it outside of marriage. When you remain sexually involved with your spouse, you are consenting to, participating in, and in many ways perpetuating false intimacy. A hiatus on sexual activity may be absolutely essential for both you and your spouse in order to enable you both to explore complex emotions and deal with the deeper problems in your marriage.

Choosing to abstain from sexual relations is the direct opposite of withdrawing from the relationship. This choice is not made in anger or to gain revenge, but in loving commitment to work toward restoration. When you choose not to have sexual relations, your spouse may experience isolation and shame, and consequently feel despair that can lead to seeking God fervently (see Hosea 3). You withhold sexual relations so that "the sinful nature may be destroyed" (1 Corinthians 5:5) and "in order that [he or she] may feel ashamed" (2 Thessalonians 3:14).

Your incentive to live in this manner must go far beyond improving your marital relationship. Such a goal is woefully inadequate; the risks inherent in this choice are too high for such a motive. Only the compelling love of the Savior who offers more of Himself to you, and the hope and desire to see your spouse rescued from sin, can sustain you during this difficult time. Withholding sex should not be an impulsive act. It requires preparation, prayer, and the support of other Christians who fully understand the objectives of your decision. (See appendix A, page 195, for further reading on this subject.)

Feelings of Guilt

On learning the extent of your addicted spouse's behavior, you may have strong feelings of guilt. "If only I had been more sexually available . . . had cared more about having sex . . . this wouldn't have happened." If you are feeling guilty, recognize that you aren't the primary cause of the sexual addiction and therefore shouldn't feel "false guilt."

Your spouse may even appeal to your sense of false guilt to justify his or her behavior. Some addicted persons have responded to their spouse's knowledge of their addiction by proclaiming, "God has healed me" or "God can heal me better than any therapist could." This puts tremendous pressure on their spouses by attempting to manipulate them into going along—otherwise, it appears as if the spouses are questioning what God is doing in the addicted person's life, or doubting God's ability to heal. But that's just the sex addict's way of denying the seriousness of his or her problems and covering up a failure to pursue God with brokenness and passion.

Are you feeling guilty? Granted, you may have done or said things that impacted sexual expression in your marriage. Probably, you need to look closely at your responses to your addicted spouse and be willing to make changes. But don't allow guilt to minimize the extent and consequences of your spouse's addiction. Lack of sexual interest isn't a primary cause of sexual addiction. Typically, the causes go back to adolescence and deep spiritual issues. Your spouse may have been involved in some form of sexually addictive behavior long before you two even met.

Instead of focusing on your guilt, concentrate on whatever you can do to support your spouse emotionally and guide him or her toward restoration. If your feelings of guilt continue, you should talk with a counselor who can help you work through them and discover the hope and inner peace that God offers you.

TAKE CONSTRUCTIVE ACTION
Like many spouses in your situation, you may fear that if you begin to address this problem your marriage will fall apart and you'll be abandoned and rejected by your spouse and other people. You may feel deep shame and guilt.

However, the sexual addiction is what is destroying you spiritually and emotionally, negatively impacting your marriage and family, and perhaps creating much more damage than you realize. The internal damage that is taking place inside you, your spouse, and other family members or victims is quite destructive. So it's important to stop ignoring the problem, try to save your marriage, and put an end to the rising costs of sexual addiction.

Many women who are married to sex addicts are very dependent on their husbands. They're afraid of being abandoned and find it hard to trust their own judgment. Their husbands, often the "authority figures," control many aspects of their lives, including the finances. So the wives feel inadequate to challenge their behaviors.

One young woman, for instance, had been ill for quite a while and needed surgery. While she was in the hospital, her husband came to visit and brought a girlfriend along. Concerned about the extended period of recovery she was facing, she was reluctant to confront her husband about why he was seeing another woman. As it turns out, the husband rationalized that, given his wife's long-term sickness, he had the right to have a physical relationship with someone else. So his wife, who felt guilty for depriving him of sex, sought to avoid confrontation at nearly all costs.

If you don't intervene and assist your spouse in receiving help, the consequences most likely will become even worse. Your marriage will continue to suffer. Your children may be affected, whether or not molestation is actually taking place. Other children and adults may be harmed. More disease may be spread. And so on. Left to itself, your spouse's addiction won't get better. So let's examine practical steps you can take to start you and your spouse toward restoration and healing in your relationship with God and each other.

Step One: Immediately Seek Professional Counseling
If the Behavior Is Intrusive

Perhaps you learned that your spouse was sexually addicted when the police called to say that he or she had been arrested for child molestation or for peeping in someone's window. In this case, the authorities are probably determining the extent of your spouse's addictive behaviors and discovering who else may have been affected by them.

The odds are, however, that your spouse's behaviors aren't well known. Maybe you're the only one who knows. Maybe you've been suspicious for a while and only recently figured things out. The most important question now is whether or not your spouse's behavior has been intrusive.

If you know or strongly suspect that your spouse is involved in intrusive behaviors (see chapter 2) that have victimized one or more people, don't minimize his or her addictive behaviors or deny the depth of the problem. Seek the support, guidance, and objectivity of a professional counselor who will help you take the courageous steps necessary to address this seemingly insurmountable and scary problem.

There are many reasons why you should go directly into counseling, even before discussing the sexual addiction with your spouse. Intrusive sexual behaviors are complex and can rarely be solved without professional treatment. They can also have serious consequences to you, to your family, and to others. Laws may have been broken, causing the legal system to become involved. The whole intensity of the situation may escalate rapidly.

When you take action, you may feel as if you are tearing your life apart, and you will need the support of a counselor. You may feel almost like a prosecutor in a courtroom, even though your goal is to help your spouse overcome his or her addiction. Your world will be shaken up and turned upside down. In addition, your spouse has many reasons for hiding his or her intrusive behavior from others, including fears of serious legal, financial, and relational consequences. Your spouse may do almost anything to avoid being "caught," including the possibility of using physical force or threats against you.

Step Two: Take Steps to Intervene So the Problems Can Be Resolved

It's vital that your spouse receive professional counseling for intrusive and/or nonintrusive sexually addictive behaviors. Through a carefully planned intervention, you may be able to play a key role in helping your spouse (who may seem to be involved only in nonintrusive behaviors) recognize the seriousness of the problem and choose to receive help.

What do I mean by an intervention? It's a meeting between you and your spouse in which you (or your counselor) carry out a carefully planned sequence of steps designed to motivate your spouse to seek professional counseling. It's a time when you attempt to discuss the sexually addictive problems with your spouse, show support, and communicate in a firm but loving way that he or she must deal with the addiction through counseling.

Although there are no perfect, universal steps for responding to a problem as complex as sexual addiction, the following guidelines will help you carry out a successful intervention. As you think them through, evaluate how well they apply to your situation. Remain flexible, ready to move to a different approach if necessary.

PREPARING AN INTERVENTION
Choose a Counselor Ahead of Time

If you know the degree of sexually addictive behavior in which your spouse has been or is still involved, find a counselor who is familiar with the dynamics of that specific behavior. For instance, if your spouse has sexually molested children, the counselor should have professional experience with families in which there is ongoing sexual abuse (not just adult victims of sexual abuse), knowledge of the dynamics of incestuous families, and skills in dealing with victimized children.

As part of the identification process, feel free to ask the counselor which books he or she has read on sexual addiction and which courses he or she has taken in addition to graduate-level courses. If you have already been meeting with a professional counselor and are pleased with this person, there's probably no reason to change counselors unless he or she is unable to provide the help with sexual addiction that you and your spouse may require.

It's important to rely on a Christian counselor, whenever possible, who not only understands the Bible and what it says about the nature of life and people but also comprehends the complexities of sexually addictive behavior. In many areas of the country, there are few Christian counselors who understand these complexities. Many people can't deal with sexually addictive behavior due to lack of training or understanding. If you find this to be true in your area, find a Christian friend who will encourage and support you through the tough times. Later, that person may need to help you find a professional counselor — Christian or nonChristian — who has worked with sexually addicted people.

Don't simply pick a counselor out of the telephone directory. Check with trusted friends or close family members who can keep a confidence about whether they have heard about or know of a counselor whose professionalism is respected. The best recommendations often come from others who have received help from a counselor, or from pastors and lay counselors who refer people to professionals when there are problems that require specialized training.

Focus on the Purpose of the Confrontation

If after talking with the counselor you decide to intervene on your spouse's behalf, you must be committed to your spouse above all else. What he or she is doing may make you livid. But you still need to approach your spouse in love and be able and willing to express compassion, not criticism.

Remember, your spouse probably feels more guilt and shame about this behavior than you can ever imagine. Your spouse's worst fear may be that you would find out. So be as supportive, sympathetic, and understanding as you can during the intervention, laying a framework of trust and love. Also keep in mind that the vast majority of sex addicts are victims of child abuse—frequently sexual abuse. Your spouse has made wrong choices, but other factors may have deeply affected those choices. Recognize that, but for the grace of God, you might be involved in similar behavior.

This doesn't mean you should condone what your spouse is doing. It *does* mean that your love is deep enough to enable you to envision your spouse being freed from sexual addiction and to long for that day in spite of what is now occurring. This is usually difficult, especially when you feel that the addictive behavior has damaged your life and the lives of others. You will need extra time to reflect on your motives for bringing up the issues of sexual addiction and for recommitting yourself to your marriage, unless there's a risk of physical harm to you and your family.

Gain the Prayerful Support of Others

Loving intervention is a necessity, not an option. God calls us to confront others who are involved in sinful behavior, and this may be one of the toughest interventions you'll ever face. Pray and ask God for His wisdom. Search the Scriptures for guidance. If you are already in counseling, rely on the counselor for assistance. If a Christian friend can assist you in your preparation, seek him or her out. Without revealing the nature or extent of the problem, ask others to pray for you as you "face a difficult time."

No matter what other facts influence the discussion you will soon have with your spouse, always remember this: *The main reason for your intervention will be to encourage your spouse to obtain the help he or she needs.* As long as you have a relationship that can be salvaged, you will basically want to communicate to your spouse, "I'm committed to you, to seeing your life restored, to strengthening our relationship together, to getting closer to you and God in a stronger spiritual relationship."

Check Your Insurance Coverage

Unfortunately, professional counseling is usually expensive. If you have insurance, evaluate your plan and discuss any general issues with the insurance company representative or insurance facilitator at your place of business. If the counseling is just too expensive for you, with or without insurance, check with the counselor anyway. Some counselors will agree to provide services at a reduced charge or can refer you to someone else whose services cost less.

Carefully Choose the Time and Place

Knowing how you and your spouse typically communicate about difficult issues will help you determine the ideal setting in which you both can discuss the sexual addiction.

For example, don't consider discussing these issues at eleven o'clock at night when you're both tired, an hour before one of you has to leave on a trip, or just before your child returns from school. You'll need hours in which you can discuss problems, feelings, fears, and difficult issues.

Try to find out whether your spouse will be home at a certain time so you can plan the time of the intervention. "Will you be home at the usual time this evening? I have several things to talk over with you." "What time should we plan on dinner?" "What's your schedule this evening?" Don't tell your spouse ahead of time what you plan to discuss.

Invite a Third Person If Circumstances Warrant

If addressing difficult issues with your spouse has ever resulted in physical harm to you or other family members, or if you or your spouse suffer from some type of illness that could affect your ability to respond or communicate appropriately when the discussion gets heated, arrange for the presence of a third person during the intervention to ensure safety and help in other ways. If you haven't done so already, seek out a professional counselor who can advise you on the best ways to proceed.

If a third person is needed, consider these general qualifications:

- Someone who isn't a professional counselor or pastor and won't intimidate your spouse. (However, if you and your spouse have been or are currently in counseling, it may be appropriate to invite that counselor or use him or her as a guiding resource.)
- Someone your spouse knows, respects, and trusts.
- Someone who is willing to read parts of this book ahead of time.
- Someone who will maintain confidentiality.
- A strong friend who believes in you and your marriage and will encourage you to address the issues.
- Someone "neutral" who will guide the discussion out of a rut or away from overly emotional responses.
- Someone who doesn't overreact emotionally to issues and can remain calm and perceptive.
- Someone who can demonstrate compassion toward your spouse and not simply moralize the whole situation and use the meeting as a chance to preach.
- Ideally, someone who has a vibrant faith in God.

Consider the Children

If you have children living at home, arrange for them to be away with a friend or relative when you and your spouse talk seriously about the sexual addiction. They shouldn't overhear what you both discuss and shouldn't be put in the middle of a situation that could become intense. Even if you choose a time when they are asleep, your discussion could awaken them and cause trauma if they suddenly walk into the room and overhear what is said.

Recognize that Everything Can't Be Solved at Once

Whether your spouse's behavior is intrusive, nonintrusive, or a combination of both, the internal and external factors leading to the behavior are complex. They didn't develop overnight. It will take time for you and your spouse to work things through. This is just the first step.

BEGINNING THE INTERVENTION

As you begin the discussion, indicate that you are aware that your spouse has a problem with sexual behavior that can't be ignored. Don't allow the focus to shift to whether or not there's a problem. This isn't the time to convince your spouse that he or she has a problem. It *is* the time to say that something needs to be done about the behavior.

The following guidelines may help you remain more sensitive to your spouse and be prepared for surprises that could come up during the intervention.

Realize the Problem May Be Bigger Than You Think

Perhaps your spouse has been involved in sexually addictive behaviors that you know nothing about. When you begin the conversation, indicate that you're aware that there's a problem and that you are concerned about it. Emphasize lovingly that you need to know the full extent of the problem in order to help. By asking your spouse to divulge what the problem is rather than assuming that you know the full extent of the behavior, you may learn more.

Don't Overreact

As you become aware of the types of sexually addictive behavior your spouse has used and how long they have been going on, you may feel overwhelmed with pain and be tempted either to lash out or to withdraw. Work hard to speak clearly without raising your voice. Raised voices have a way of escalating intensity unnecessarily. If you can't receive the information from your spouse without arguing, becoming angry and hurtful, or withdrawing, end the discussion quickly and contact a professional counselor who can help you deal with your own feelings as well as the sexually addictive behaviors of your spouse.

Avoid Simplistic Judgments

Saying something like, "You simply have to get right with God and do what He says in the Bible," is inappropriate. Remember, this isn't the time to try to solve the problems. It's only a time to discuss them and encourage your spouse to obtain professional help.

Be Prepared for Defensive Behavior

Each person responds to stressful situations in individual ways, particularly such a personal issue as sexually addictive behavior. One spouse may tend to withdraw and become depressed; another spouse may become defensive and abusive. Yet another may listen, discuss, admit wrongdoing, and be relieved that his or her actions are finally out in the open. Some sex addicts may even become suicidal because they're so ashamed. Again, emphasize that you're "there" for your spouse, that you will help, and that you care deeply for him or her.

If your spouse becomes violent, end the discussion immediately. If the anger is more than just a passing emotion, you (and any young children) may need to even leave home or contact a professional counselor or the police to ensure your own safety.

If your spouse mentions suicide, take it seriously and quickly contact a professional counselor. If one isn't available, contact a pastor, the social services department, or your spouse's best friend. Such a threat indicates that your spouse needs prompt assistance. If after the mention of suicide your spouse seems almost happy, be concerned. It may be that he or she is simply relieved to have made the decision to die.

Evaluate Your Spouse's Response

If your spouse agrees that he or she needs help, gently encourage but don't pressure him or her to receive counseling right away. Be sensitive to how your spouse feels about seeing a counselor. Realize that this prospect may seem terrifying.

If your spouse completely denies that the problem exists or says it's not severe enough to bother about, recognize that many sex addicts are oblivious to the true quality of their relationships and frequently rationalize many issues that require serious attention. Your spouse may even exclaim, "You're insane, just imagining things! How could you possibly think such horrible things about me?!"

If this happens, lovingly and tactfully end the conversation. You could say something like, "It deeply saddens me that you don't want to address this issue honestly. I don't care to argue or convince you about this. We'll need to talk about it another time." Then contact a professional counselor or pastor who has had some experience with sex addicts. There's nothing to be gained at this point if your spouse won't admit the problem, and your counselor will help you evaluate how to respond in ways that may influence your spouse to consider dealing with the sexual addiction in the future.

SUMMARY

Many aspects of our culture emphasize the importance of meeting our own needs first before addressing the needs of others. As I conclude this chapter, my great concern is that spouses of sex addicts who move toward getting help may begin to justify self-centeredness as they deal with the tough challenges presented by sexual addiction. Or they may do nothing about the addiction and simply "forgive" their spouses, using "spiritual" approaches that may be little more than fearful reactions and further attempts to handle life in ways that maintain levels of comfort. Neither response will result in the level of healing and restoration that God offers and that countless people have received.

If you are dealing with your marriage partner's sexual addiction, it's my prayer that you will examine your heart, challenge the fortress of self-protection and evidences of false intimacy in your own life, and allow yourself to be drawn closer to a personal relationship with God. Only then will you be able to respond effectively during this difficult time and express the love of God to others—even to your addicted spouse who has failed to love you.

A word of caution: This chapter is only a summary of some of the issues that a spouse may face in dealing with sexual addiction. It is not comprehensive or exhaustive. It is highly recommended that you consider consultation with a professional therapist and/or attorney who is experienced in this area before you confront a spouse with this problem.

✛ 6 ✛

Preventing Sexual Addiction in Your Children

I write this chapter reluctantly because of my concern that some parents won't focus long enough on it and those who aren't parents may wrongly assume that they don't need to read it. Others might read this chapter first and, not finding instant solutions, ignore the rest of the book.

Please take time to think about and apply the following material. Written to parents (and others, too), this section explores how your relationship with God can be a vital factor in reducing the likelihood of sexual addiction developing in your children. This chapter also suggests practical ways in which you can make a difference in children's lives.

PARENTING WITHOUT GUARANTEES

If someone walked up to me and asked, "How can I keep my kids from developing sexually addictive behavior?" I'd be hard pressed to give a concise answer. Why? People who have honestly struggled with life know deep in their hearts that parenting formulas don't always work.

If all parents had to do was to manage their children's external environment—the neighborhood they live in, the schools they attend, the friends they choose, the quality of parenting they experience—

parenting would be relatively elementary. A solid understanding of child development, a knowledge of effective parenting principles, and just plain common sense would go even further in making children's lives go smoothly. But parenting involves far more than controlling a child's environment.

During my graduate studies in educational psychology, I specialized in parenting education. My motives for this direction were professional and personal: I wanted to take the courses required for clinical membership in the American Association of Marriage and Family Therapy, and I also wanted to learn how to be a better parent.

As I look back on those courses, I realize I did learn quite a bit. But I cringe at the thought of a parenting expert presenting "ten steps to effective parenting." Everyone knows that parenting can't be reduced to standardized formulas.

Step-by-step procedures are a great help in assembling a new bicycle, but they don't work in preventing sexual addiction. Nothing will guarantee that our children will turn out the way we hope. Obviously, we love our children and want to see them grow to maturity and live productive lives. We want them to have fine educations, good marriages, and fulfilling careers. As believers, we long to see them walk with the Lord. But we can't protect our children from all the serious problems in this sinful world. Likewise, if the causes of sexual addiction aren't just external and therefore can't simply be correlated to such factors as severe family dysfunction or child abuse, merely improving the external workings of our families won't dramatically decrease the rate of sexual addiction.

Sexual addiction, as we've seen, is symptomatic of sin deep in the heart, and preventing sin is impossible. That's why we must focus first on our own relationship with God. Any attempt to prevent sexual addiction in our children that isn't founded on our relationship with God is pretentious. Without such a focus, our attempts to deal with the complexities of sexual addiction are as futile as applying tiny bandages to seriously wounded patients.

DEVELOP A VIBRANT RELATIONSHIP WITH GOD
Most of us have been told, at one time or another, to "get right with the Lord." All too frequently this is used as a cliché in an attempt to avoid, deny, or minimize issues. But the truth is, we can reduce

the possibility of sexual addiction in our children by developing a vibrant relationship with the Lord that positively impacts not only our relationships with our children but their own relationship with God. (I'm not simply referring to more church involvement, attending more Bible studies, and implementing family devotions. I'm talking about developing a personal relationship with God that goes far deeper than activities.)

If you come away from this chapter with only one critical point, remember this: *Each of us must pursue godliness with everything we have.* Healthy living within a family and in relationship requires rich and passionate dependence on God. Our children experience and learn these dynamics from us.

Even when we do our best to know God and allow Him to impact the quality of our relationships with our children, bad things can happen to them. During reflective moments, we know that things in our world aren't right. Tension and disappointment come with the territory. Sometimes we try to alter the factors in our external world to avoid the effects of sin and make life more appealing. We change our surroundings, develop new or healthier relationships, schedule more family time, or simply go on vacation. But good family activities can't diminish the impact of the sin that rages within us and our children.

We want and need more loving relationships, but often our motives and the paths we use to find fulfillment and deepen connections seem confusing and impractical. Even developing better relationships with our children can't be our ultimate goal, for improved relationships are the fruits of godly living cultivated as we uncover the filthiness of our hearts and turn to God in humble surrender. Such exposure and forgiveness of sin ripens the blameless character that produces love. The path toward Christlikeness is through a deepening realization that our hearts are wicked and will try to lead us away from trusting the Lord completely. Concentrating on the reality of sin rather than on the external qualities of family life is the most effective parenting tool in preventing sexual addiction.

WE MUST DEAL FIRST WITH OUR OWN BEHAVIOR

Much of the way we interact with our children is automatic, resulting from our self-centered way of approaching relationships. Therefore it's important for us to examine ourselves seriously, to look at the ways we relate to God, to our children, and to other people. The patterns of interaction that take place between the sex addict and his or her "partner" in the sexual fantasy in many ways mirror the interaction we establish between ourselves and our children. The patterns of detachment, withdrawal, and avoiding disappointment that are common in sex addicts often begin in childhood as children learn to model what their parents do.

In my counseling, I've observed that many parents are more interested in focusing on problems their children experience than on focusing on their own problems. One reason for this is that children's problems, at times, feel less complex and more manageable than our own. We'd rather have a sense that we are accomplishing something — helping to manage a child's difficulty — than face our own problems. Serious and courageous self-examination of the intent of our own hearts and the goals of our relationships with our children is one of the most difficult tasks any parent can perform. The Bible commends it as part of godly living: "A wicked man puts up a bold front, but an upright man gives thought to his ways" (Proverbs 21:29).

One of my great deficiencies as a parent is that when I experience disappointments, just as my child experiences disappointments, I find myself trying to pretend that my relationships aren't really as bad as they are. As a result, I can easily attempt to create the same illusion for my child that relationships aren't painful. Then, when the inevitable pain of relationships catches up with my child, he or she experiences even greater pain and possibly disillusionment, because I haven't modeled how to deal with reality in a God-honoring way.

To face what is happening in my heart that causes me to create this illusion, I must first look at the illusions I create of my parenting skills. Do I depend on my skills and my relationships with my children to control my children's relationship with their world? If so, I'm creating an illusion that life is much easier than it really is, rather than helping them understand and face relational pain. By trying to spare them (and myself) inevitable disappointment, I can be a block in their pursuit of God as the only source of real meaning.

Am I willing to examine the ways that I move toward my children as a result of my own self-centeredness and self-protection? Can I look at my own failure to love and how I've attempted to create a safe relationship with a child who is easier to mold and direct than other adults in my life? This is a difficult truth for me, and I suspect for most parents, to face.

There are some disturbing, direct parallels between what I try to do as a parent to create a safe relationship with my child and what a sex addict attempts to do in using a prostitute or a glossy photograph to create the illusion of relational safety. In a subtle way, we both may be depending ultimately on our own resources to make relationships work, and so creating an illusion that disregards God.

When we evaluate our parent-child relationship, we may recognize that the way we relate to our children apparently teaches them not to rely on anyone but themselves. If so, we must also recognize that a serious problem within us must be addressed and that we can't do that by ourselves.

We each need to ask honestly:

- Is my primary goal with my children to do everything I can to help them avoid failure and achieve success as they grow through adolescence and into adulthood?
- How emotionally detached from my children am I? Am I focusing too much on external issues?
- Am I able to move toward my children's pain as they grapple with getting good grades in school, finding acceptance from friends, or trying to make the team? Or am I afraid that doing so will make me aware of my own fears and failures as a parent?
- Do I deal with the agony I feel as I sense the agony my children sometimes feel, or do I back away from my children's agony because I can't face the pain within myself?
- Do I back away from the tough issues? Am I content simply to be a "good parent" and meet my children's material needs?
- Because I'm afraid of pain and disappointment, am I somehow putting a sense of obligation on my children, in which they feel that the only way they can be acceptable to me is to succumb to the pressure to succeed and make me feel good?
- Have I experienced such pain and disappointment in my own relationships that I make my children feel that

they desperately need me and that I'm essential to their
achievement?

- Do I find myself giving so much to my job that I have little or
nothing emotionally to give to my children? Am I avoiding
intimacy?
- Can my children feel free to really reveal to me what they are
thinking and doing, without fear of rejection?
- Am I willing to trust God with my pain and disappointment,
to allow Him to be the source of ultimate fulfillment in my
life? Will I submit to Him all my desires and my needs for
relationship?

We must deal with our own unfulfilled desires before we can be of
great spiritual help to our children. If our desires lack a biblical direction, we can't sincerely encourage our children to pursue that direction.
Each of us must ask ourselves penetrating questions that can reveal
unhealthy ways we respond to other people. These questions include:

- How do I deal with the desire to be loved?
- How do I relate to others when I feel alone?
- Do I gain love and acceptance by always being helpful
and kind?
- Do I avoid conflict in order to be liked or to remain in
control?
- Am I afraid to contemplate my own hurt?
- Do I feel lonely? If so, how do I deal with my loneliness?
- Do I get angry? If so, when? If not, why not?
- Do I often take charge, wanting to lead, even though inside
I'd rather not?
- Do I trust someone enough to let him or her know my deep-
est feelings?
- How often do I share my true thoughts and feelings with
others?
- Do I intimidate others to gain control?
- Do I find it difficult to make decisions?
- Am I suspicious of people's motives?
- Do I have little interest in sex?
- Do I use sex to gain power?

■ Am I flirtatious and seductive with others?
■ Do I feel uncomfortable with or distrust compliments?
■ Am I impulsive in my commitments to others?
■ Do I cause conflict to avoid continuing relationships?
■ Am I easily hurt often?

As best you can, evaluate your answers to these questions honestly. Then make the commitment to begin dealing with the areas in which you are weak.

ACKNOWLEDGE THAT TRUE FULFILLMENT COMES ONLY FROM GOD

Our responsibilities as parents are in some ways overwhelming. In his book *Parenting Adolescents*, Kevin Huggins stated, "The inevitable result of personal reflection in light of the Scriptures is an erosion of the parent's confidence in his own ability to make life work for himself and his children."[1] We can't effectively parent (or do anything to prevent sexual addiction in our children) unless we are willing to develop a deep understanding of the nature of our own relationships and how they impact our children. Our recognition of that fact can motivate us to depend more on our heavenly Father and the Body of Christ for encouragement and support in our weaknesses. Or it can drive us on a godless quest for self-fulfillment that can keep us from developing genuine intimacy with our children and thereby fail to model what it means to know God. Ultimately, we need to understand our tendency to adamantly refuse to become more dependent on God. We can't parent well unless we passionately understand that He is the source of true fulfillment.

As we interact with people, we are motivated to fulfill our desires and needs by using different strategies. If we don't move toward God and others in genuine love, we are motivated by other pretenses, other motives, and other reasons for doing what we do. We develop styles or patterns of interaction that manipulate others to respond in the ways we want them to respond. Sometimes we use indirect methods to obtain what we want because we simply don't believe that anyone would ever want to give us the desires of our heart. We know that the pain of disappointment, humiliation, and rejection is inevitable and that someone will say no or block our attempts to pursue a goal at least some of the time. So we find various ways to numb our relational pain or satisfy our desires safely.

However, as parents we are always being watched: Our children learn by observing us. If we avoid relationships, withdraw, pout, get angry, show kindness, or do special favors in order to obtain what we want, our children may learn to do that, too. Likewise, if we express our desires through direct, sincere requests and are willing to face relational pain, our children may be more willing to enter the relational uncertainty in which real intimacy can develop.

Are we willing to acknowledge the complexity of life and relationships, feel the inevitable confusion, and know that we are helpless to control what's really happening to our children internally? Will we acknowledge the tenacity with which we move sinfully in our own directions and then seek fulfillment in God? Will we allow God's power to course through us so we can be free to love others without ever requiring that they'll love us in return?

If so, there is great hope that our parenting efforts will succeed. There is hope that our desires for meaningful relationships—and those of our children—can be met. There's hope that our relationships with our children can be improved. When we depend on God, realizing that no magic formula can guarantee that our children will develop healthy relationships and flee false intimacy, we have hope.

To look at prevention this way isn't easy. It forces us to evaluate what's really going on in our hearts and in our family relationships. It's easy to think that we as parents are doing enough. But as we'll see, the seeds of future sexual addiction can be sown even in Christian families that appear to be doing rather well.

As children grow and physically mature, they are naturally motivated to thirst for things that will satisfy their needs and provide protection from pain. They often crave a source that they perceive will be a fountain of life-giving fulfillment. As parents, we may be tempted to satisfy these desires with external things, believing that hunger pangs are unhealthy. But we must understand that we're incapable of filling our children's internal hunger. Part of our job as parents is to help our children recognize their internal desires and then guide them toward a fulfilling relationship with God. Otherwise their deep desires, combined with their natural inclination to pursue self-gratification and avoid pain, will inevitably lead our children toward evil.

While I was growing up, my understanding of a person's relationship with God was shaped in terms of lifestyle: no dancing, no movies, no makeup, etc. But there's much more to knowing God than clean living, Bible reading, obeying God-honoring rules, and consistent Sunday school attendance. Until we parents face life honestly, worshiping and knowing God are like empty clichés. Knowing God intimately results only when we acknowledge that we can't make everything turn out all right on our own. But this humility goes against our nature and is therefore hard to accept.

During a workshop in Dallas several years ago, I pointed out that life is often not within our control and that accepting that fact scares us. A lady interrupted me to say, "You mean, if I live as God desires, serving Him and living a Christian life, what matters most to me may not work out as I want?"

"Yes," I answered. "That's exactly what I'm saying."

Her surprisingly candid response was, "Well, that stinks!"

God's grace extended to us never has real meaning until we admit that we're beaten. Pretending that we can control life sustains false intimacy in relationships, whether they are between parents and their children, marriage partners, or clients and prostitutes. When we admit our helplessness and stand naked, ashamed, helpless, and trembling before God, His abiding love impacts our very nature and at that point we "taste" His goodness. God's amazing grace will then excite us and motivate us to love the way He does.

As parents, we each must ask, "Do my kids know the thrill of being in this kind of relationship with God? Do I attempt to demonstrate this relationship with my children and therefore reflect Christ? In what I say and do, are my kids beginning to learn that they can't improve the quality of their lives without God?"

The danger here is not that our children will discover their deepest longings, but that they will attempt to fulfill their unmet longings on their own without relying on God. If we don't recognize our children's desires and help them wrestle with the causes and consequences of those desires, other people will do it for them. The result? In most cases children are left to grapple with pain, disappointment, and confusion. When children search for ways to cope with their unfulfilled desires without the guidance of parents who love God, they are vulnerable prey to the lurking false intimacy of sexual addiction.

CHANGING PARENTING STYLES

I can hear it now: "Okay, you're right. I *am* dealing with tough issues in my life that affect the way I relate to my kids. So what do I do?"

Changing parenting styles essentially requires the same internal process a sex addict must go through to leave his or her addiction. Each of us must courageously and completely remove anything that locks us into patterns of relationships that ultimately don't honor God and that keep us from acknowledging Him as the source of all deep meaning. It's a difficult, taxing process that begins with self-evaluation.

Once we identify how deeply we are motivated by inner fears and how those fears influence our actions toward our children and other people, we can begin to make choices that will help us learn to live and love according to God's ways. We can move toward our children, not to meet our own needs, but to find greater fulfillment through self-sacrifice and love. When we begin to move toward our children in this way, when our primary goal is to love them and share their pain, we'll become even more aware of how we lack the real ability to love our children as God calls us to love them. As we begin to feel how inadequate we are as parents, we will focus more on who we are, what's going on in our lives, and on our relationship with God.

Of all the relationships in which we're involved, the parent/child relationship is the one in which we must be most willing to endure pain and disappointment. Only through our willingness to love vulnerably, which stems from our faith in God, do we grow in character and provide the greatest possible spiritual benefits to our children. Essentially we need to apply Jesus' words in Luke 9:24 — "Whoever wants to save his life will lose it, but whoever loses his life for me will save it."

To remain highly motivated to be involved with our children and to touch their pain, we essentially must be committed to self-denial and self-sacrifice. First Peter 2:21-23 presents a challenge to us as parents:

> To this you were called, because Christ suffered for you, leaving you an example, that you should follow in his steps.
> "He committed no sin,
>   and no deceit was found in his mouth."
> When they hurled their insults at him, he did not retaliate; when he suffered, he made no threats. Instead, he entrusted himself to him who judges justly.

Relational disappointment is inevitable in a fallen world. Our children will disappoint us; we'll disappoint them. My wife and I have two sons. One has a learning disability; the other was born with a cleft lip and palate and other physical problems. I find, to my shame, how easy it is to want to withdraw from the pain. Each day as I interact with them, I'm aware of the chronic challenges they face and the crushing disappointment I feel. I've never entertained the thought of leaving my family, but a part of me wants to run as far away from the agony as possible. At times, internally, I hang by what feels like a thread on the knowledge that God's love constrains me to love as He loves me.

Peter is calling all of us to move toward others, including our children, with a deep conviction that only God can meet the deepest desires of our hearts. We then become free from the demand that our children meet our desires and can take whatever relational risks are necessary to encourage them to enter a trusting relationship with God—their heavenly Father. When we're willing to take these risks, we'll greatly influence them to move toward God, not toward things that seem to promise a happy life.

THE IMPORTANCE OF AN INTIMATE PARENT/CHILD RELATIONSHIP

As parents or others in positions of leadership, it's our responsibility to nurture the children under our care in the best ways possible. As we saw in chapter 3, fear of intimacy, feelings of abandonment, lack of appreciation, loneliness, and other internal factors help create fertile ground for sexually addictive behavior. Conversely, when a parent is able to establish a positive model of what it means to struggle with the uncertainty of relational intimacy, the child's chances of developing sexually addictive behavior are greatly reduced.

If a child receives little acceptance and appreciation while growing up and for one reason or another never experiences an intimate relationship with a parent, that doesn't mean that the child will grow up to be a sex addict. It does mean, however, that he or she will probably struggle with the uncertainty of intimacy and pursue a more secure direction with the illusion of control. Each child makes his or her choices about how to respond to loneliness, abandonment, and relational disappointment. Two children, for example, could experience the same kind of abuse and neglect at early ages, and one might choose sexually addictive behaviors while the other will not.

Where do adolescents who are experiencing a new capacity for relationships turn when they become disillusioned and the world becomes lonelier? Do they turn to their parents? To their peer group? Withdraw into themselves? Young people naturally search for ways to avoid pain and gain fulfillment. Relationships with others play a vital role in this search. Peers help them learn who they are. Adults, especially parents, serve as role models. But like all of us, children reflect their deepest motives when they approach and cultivate relationships.

A child who knows God and feels loved is more likely to take a risky step toward developing an intimate relationship than one who has learned the hard way that intimacy leads to pain. The more committed to self-protection a child is, the more likely it is that he or she will hold back in relationships for fear of being hurt, thereby creating more internal pain. Failure in relationships reinforces the seeming advantages of painless fantasy—the self-created illusion of being accepted. This, in turn, can begin the cycle of sexual addiction.

Many teenagers assume that suspicion, jealousy, dependence, and possessiveness are normal in relationships because that's what they've experienced at home. So they begin to isolate themselves from relational pain and trust in themselves for fulfillment. Feeling that they aren't really good enough to attract someone worth loving, they learn to manipulate others by misrepresenting who they are. They put on a "false front" and hide behind it. Some teenagers do anything to get a relationship going because they fear being alone, or they try to control others to get what they need.

Ultimately, relational approaches that aren't based on love lead only to more pain and a further commitment to self-protection, which may feed back into the illusion of gaining fulfillment through sexually addictive behaviors.

PRACTICAL WAYS TO BUILD INTIMATE RELATIONSHIPS WITH CHILDREN

In the remaining part of this chapter, we'll look at other areas that contribute to building intimate relationships with our children and thereby help prevent sexually addictive behavior from developing. But these guidelines are of little value unless we've first grappled with our patterns of relating to our children and to God.

We must remember that just being good parents and doing the right things won't make everything okay. Our children won't escape all the pain and temptations of life. But if we face our weaknesses and pain and depend on God for fulfillment, we can be strong spiritual role models for our children and help them learn how to choose real intimacy rather than false intimacy.

With the above points in mind, let's look at specific ways that you—and other family members or concerned adults—can help prevent the seeds of sexual addiction from germinating in your children. Let's look at how you can build a parental foundation on healthy communication, love, and acceptance. This foundation can help shield your children from the feelings of abandonment, loneliness, and rejection that can lead to sexually addictive behaviors.

Some of the following guidelines may seem familiar because they apply to more than the prevention of sexual addiction. At first they may seem too simplistic to you. But keep in mind that children who are learning to trust in God more than themselves and who have learned to deal with intimacy and relational pain will be better prepared to develop intimate relationships and handle the rejections and disappointments of life. How we as parents respond to our children's needs—for example, how we help our children work through the pain and disappointments inherent in relationships—is a crucial part of the prevention process.

Create an Environment Where Your Child Can
Share Desires Safely

Sadly, all children operate in what could be termed a hostile world. At school, for example, children make cruel comments and routinely accept or reject one another. Thus every child will invariably come home from school with a complaint, feeling frustrated, anxious, and fearful of rejection. Obviously, how you (or another close family member) respond to what the child is experiencing can greatly shape his or her view of intimacy, relationships, and God.

For example, if your child comes home from school and says, "Kara says she doesn't like me anymore and called me Freckleface," it isn't appropriate to try to make the situation better by pretending that the painful reality doesn't exist. Instead, you should respond according to your child's age in acknowledging the deep desires and the struggle to have meaningful relationships.

It's easy to respond, "Well, it doesn't matter what Kara thinks or says" and change the subject. This type of response communicates that you really don't want to talk about the subject and consider it to be insignificant. Consequently, the next time a relational difficulty occurs, your child may keep his or her feelings of loneliness and rejection buried inside.

Remember, your child's hurt and pain are real and the desire to avoid being hurt is legitimate. During a crisis time, your child will tend to move in a direction that reinforces the illusion that he or she is self-sufficient. None of us wants to face the unpredictability of relationships and our inability to make them work well. We want to believe that eventually we'll find a way to obtain satisfaction on our own. Therefore, it's important for you to offer spiritual guidance that will offset the selfish direction of your child's autonomous heart.

Sometimes a parent who learns about a child's relational problem will respond logically and lay out a number of steps the child can follow in hopes of resolving the situation (as if interpersonal difficulties can easily be solved by following certain steps). Providing guidance is an important aspect of parenting, but often what's needed goes far deeper than just giving advice. The child may not need advice on how to handle the situation; he or she may need comfort and support.

Most of all, your child needs assistance in discerning godly directions. Be willing to listen to the despair and disappointments. Realize that your child is experiencing, perhaps intensely, the consequences of living in a fallen world that hasn't met his or her deepest desires. This isn't the time to provide an escape for your child. This is a crucial time for children to learn about themselves, about what life is like, and about God. After all, they will experience relational pain time and time again.

There's no wizardry in responding to our children's pain, but we mustn't simply attempt to relieve it. We must encourage our children to explore with us how to handle the pain of their unfulfilled desires. We must give them godly alternatives, helping them to deal with their desires in godly ways. This isn't time for a sermon; it's time for sharing with your child about God's unconditional gift of love that He offers to each of us.

In adolescence, issues of uncertainty in relationships and the pain of rejection and disappointment are often related to the opposite sex. When a child reaches adolescence, it becomes clear whether or not his or her parents have successfully created a healthy relationship in which the son or daughter can share real intimacy. Can a son, for instance, share his feelings about girls with his father or mother and not feel that his feelings and the physical reactions of his body are abnormal or something to be ashamed of? Can a daughter share thoughts about her physical appearance without feeling that her parents will reject her feelings? What about the son who finds a pornographic magazine and begins to have trouble with fantasies? Will he discuss that with his father? What about the daughter who thinks her breasts are too small or the son who is being laughed at for being uncoordinated in sports?

It's important for you to communicate regularly with your child and allow him or her to safely express desires for relationships or any other area of life. This type of relationship is easier described than developed, however, because our fast-paced schedules stay packed with seemingly endless responsibilities. Obviously, our priorities are critical and need to be evaluated honestly and regularly.

Use Appropriate Physical Touch

Nearly all the sex addicts I've counseled have shared with me that their parents—or the people who raised them—were "cold," "distant," or "didn't show much affection." Through the years I've realized that appropriate physical touch plays a vital role in developing intimacy in relationships and in teaching appropriate physical boundaries, too. People tend to thrive physically and emotionally when they are nurtured with appropriate human touch. It helps to provide affirmation of love and acceptance as well as physical comfort.

Research has clearly demonstrated the relationship of appropriate physical touch to our sense of well-being and overall health. In one study, researchers divided premature babies into two groups. One group was treated according to normal protocol—isolated in an incubator with limited physical contact. The other babies were touched regularly with a human finger. The result? The babies who were touched gained weight much faster than those who weren't.

We often think of a mother hugging a son when he falls down or faces the emotional pain of rejection at school. My dad, however, also showed me physical tenderness through holding and hugs when I was hurt. Like my mother, he was there for me. When he heard I'd been injured, he'd come into the room and help bandage me or hold me. As a result, at an early age I felt that both my parents cared for me. I believe it's important for fathers to demonstrate appropriate physical affection toward their children, even if it means unlearning false notions of what it means to be male.

Model Positive Intimate Relationships

Whether they're aware of it or not, parents model what an intimate relationship is like to their children. Every day, through behaviors and attitudes, parents serve as good or bad models. There isn't much neutral ground.

The tendency in most marital relationships is for one or both to avoid dealing with issues of intimacy. Parents often live out the dynamic of wanting intimacy, but not on the other spouse's terms. A man may want to be close to his wife physically, but may not realize that the most important factor in intimacy for her is resolving day-to-day emotional issues.

At the risk of making sweeping generalizations, I'll state that in my observations, men typically back away from tough emotional issues in relationships and are fearful or reluctant to pursue intimacy. Women, on the other hand, seem to push for discussion and resolution of intimacy-related issues. I think this difference is one result of the Fall. Men try to prove that they can competently handle situations in the outside, tangible world rather than dealing with complex emotional issues.

This type of dynamic between parents teaches children volumes about intimacy—how to avoid it, that it's not worth struggling for, and that it's not vital to relationships. The curse is that all parents must continually deal with weeds and thistles cropping up in their relationships. Things do go wrong, and if parents are not prepared or equipped to handle the difficulties, it's easy to deny weakness and run away from intimacy. Marriages in which spouses can't, don't, or won't model positive aspects of intimacy won't directly cause children raised in those homes to become sex addicts. However, without the ability to recognize real intimacy, children are more vulnerable to the seductive influences of false intimacy.

Model Masculinity and Femininity

A young girl learns much about males—good or bad—from her relationship with her father. Ideally, she learns how a man should respect her, how a man can emotionally support and encourage her, and how a man can and should be able to share emotions and intimate feelings. A father's relationship with his wife (or other women if he's single) also models what it means for his daughter to have an intimate relationship with a man. Modeling goes much deeper than the subjects a father and daughter might discuss.

Every father is a model who helps his daughter learn about what her future husband may be like. Unfortunately, the main lessons some daughters learn is that some men are hurtful, insensitive, and abusive. They learn what to avoid in men rather than what to seek. Worse yet, daughters may learn that intolerable male behavior is the norm and subconsciously choose husbands who are also poor role models of what males are, thus continuing the cycle.

The same applies to the unique relationship between a son and his mother. The son needs to observe a woman who is responsive, open, caring, and supportive to him as a son and a male, not one who is negative toward men and puts them down. Appropriate modeling will help him learn what to expect in a future intimate relationship with a woman and how to approach a woman who might become his future wife.

The mother can also help her son learn to express emotions. In many families, mothers make up for fathers' inability to express feelings by showing that it's okay for their sons to express emotions. I might add at this point that many little boys find it hard to understand why they can share feelings with their mothers but that feelings make their fathers uncomfortable. Although there isn't space here to address the issue of men and their emotions, it's important for fathers to take a hard look—perhaps through others' eyes—at how well they express emotions and are willing to receive their children's emotions.

Set Appropriate Intimacy Boundaries

It's important for parents to maintain a steady intimacy boundary between themselves and their children. No child should ever have free access to everything that takes place between his or her parents.

In practical terms, this means that children should be prevented from accidentally or deliberately disrupting their parents' sexual relations. They shouldn't be permitted to hear all conversations and learn about all the problems and issues the parents are working out. Parents shouldn't constantly talk about sexual activities, openly demonstrate intimate sexual behavior in front of children, or leave pornographic materials around the house. This can give children an inappropriate sexual experience, verbally or visually, that can introduce them to sexual activities too early and lay the foundation for later sexual addiction.

Be Prudent; Not All Adults Have Pure Motives

It's evident in today's society that if parents don't provide their children with a quality of relationship, other people will develop relationships with their children that may fill the void. Good relationships may develop between peer friends, the parents of friends, or a youth pastor. Or children may seek out kids who are also lonely, feeling rejected, and trying to find what intimacy they can—healthy or not.

All too often, children who haven't experienced healthy relationships with their parents fall into the latter category and are at risk of being abused. It's important that we touch on the issue of child abuse here since sexual addiction seems to be related to child abuse, especially sexual abuse. Golden Valley Sexual Dependency Unit in Minnesota reports that more than 81 percent of the sex addicts they treat have been sexually abused.[2] The great majority have been emotionally and physically abused.

A recent article titled "Flesh Dance" in my local newspaper contained numerous quotations by strippers on why they strip for a living and the background influences that played a role in their early development. One woman said that she was sexually molested by a baby-sitter and then added, "When you're hurt like that as a child, you learn to become very mercenary with your emotions. You learn to act however you need to act to make the abuse stop. Now I guess we're learning what men like so they'll give us money."[3]

Many of the sex addicts I've treated were abused as children. Whenever I've worked with child sexual offenders—coaches, teachers, scoutmasters, youth pastors—the same themes surface. As children they felt severely abandoned and neglected. Most of them were abused sexually, and some were exposed to the horror of exploitation that left them even more deeply scarred and fearful of intimacy. Others were abused physically or emotionally—shamed, severely criticized, beaten—and simply withdrew into themselves for safety. Child sexual offenders find security and comfort in developing relationships with children because they're terrified of intimate relationships with adults.

Again, not everyone who is abused will become a sex addict. But the trauma of abuse leads a certain percentage of people to develop "safe" sexually addictive behaviors. Here are a few practical steps you can take to protect your child from abuse.

Develop a healthy caution. Many parents believe that strangers commit most acts of child abuse. When I was growing up, for instance, my parents talked about not taking a ride or candy from a stranger. But most acts of sexual molestation aren't committed by strangers; they are carried out by people—adults or teenagers—who know the children. (Golden Valley operates an in-patient unit just for teenage sex offenders!)

Stay aware of how your child relates to others, including those who are close to the family. Included in this category are: spouses, close friends, grandparents, in-laws, aunts, uncles, cousins, nieces, nephews, and baby-sitters. Concern and prudence, not fear, are in order. Isolating children isn't the answer.

The majority of people who relate to children are loving, nurturing, and truly enjoy caring for other people's children. The great majority won't sexually molest or otherwise abuse any children. Unfortunately, a few do. Some of the most qualified and gifted people in children's programs have committed child sexual abuse. Each year many children are sexually abused in youth programs—outside and inside the church. Unfortunately, it's virtually impossible to know ahead of time which youth leader or counselor is a child abuser, but there are red flags you can watch for.

Whenever a child becomes involved in a youth program, parental caution is advised. Parents must not assume that the person who is so good with children would "never do something wrong." Teenagers, too, need to learn caution. Twenty-five percent of college women have either been raped or experienced attempted rape between the ages of fourteen and twenty-one.[4]

I'm not encouraging paranoia, however. It's important for children to become involved in activities with other children and adults. They need to have the freedom to grow up, to interact, to experience various types of relationships. But parents should keep their eyes open for warning signs of abuse. (See appendix C, "Indicators of Sexual Abuse," page 199.)

Remember, too, that child molesters frequently manipulate children by providing favors, making them feel special, provoking the children's fear of losing the special relationship, or threatening them with such warnings as, "If you tell anyone, I'll hurt you or one of your family members." Children who are emotionally needy and have experienced loneliness in their families will feel more threatened by the fear of losing the relationship than will other children. To complicate things, our society encourages children to obey people in authority.

Carefully monitor the child's relational activities. Most child molesters don't move suddenly from just becoming acquainted with children to immediately molesting or sexually abusing them. There's usually a period of time in which the abusers develop the children's trust and begin to initiate activities with them that are on the borderline between appropriate and inappropriate.

Any time your child is left in the care of someone else, you should discuss with the child how that time went. If you show genuine interest, your child will generally want to share what took place. This interaction, which also builds intimacy, is a natural way to detect abuse in its initial stages, or at least to prevent ongoing abuse. But don't interrogate. Tell the child what you did when you were gone, too.

There are many questions you could ask to monitor the situation. "Were you comfortable with _____?" "What activities did you and _____ do?" "What did you play?" "What did you talk about?" Note anything suspicious in the activity. Pay attention to the child's responses. Does the child who usually loves to describe in detail what went on suddenly become quiet and reluctant to answer? If so, pay attention to the child's unwillingness and inability to report what happened. The child may simply have done something wrong and is afraid of getting into trouble. But be sure.

Be alert for any inappropriate activities. For instance, the child may have been afraid to go to bed at night and the baby-sitter said, "I'll get into bed with you." (You as a parent may do that to help the child go to sleep, but some people may question whether that's the most appropriate way to encourage desired behavior.) Find out the details of what went on. To use another example, did the baby-sitter insist on helping your child dress or undress even though the child can do that on his or her own? That's a small red flag waving.

Another warning sign is when your child becomes overly involved with or almost "worships" an older adult who has a "very special relationship" with the child, especially if that relationship is obviously quite different from the relationships the adult has with other children. Always be cautious about the "specialness" of a relationship, especially if your child spends time alone with the adult and other children don't. This level of involvement could signal a problem. The problem could intensify if the child selected for special treatment comes from an emotionally or relationally deprived situation.

To help prevent sexual abuse, always respect your child's fears of being with another person, even if it means finding another baby-sitter or giving up personal or work time. Explore what's going on and why your child may be feeling this way. Abusive adults are good at hiding their abuse. You may have to trust your child's "gut response" without any proof at all and make changes, such as switching to a different daycare or baby-sitter.

Teach children physical boundaries. Even at young ages, children should be taught about areas of their body that shouldn't be touched by someone other than a parent or physician. Young children can learn this by coloring areas that shouldn't be touched on childlike figures of people. Some parents communicate the concept that any part of the body covered by a bathing suit should never be touched.

I encourage you to talk with local educators or bookstore personnel to locate one or more of the excellent books on this topic. As children get older, they will need more specific types of descriptions regarding when touches are inappropriate and how to report them.

Provide Sex Education at an Appropriate Age

The topic of sex education remains a hot issue among Christians today. There are many articles and books with widely differing viewpoints, which I can't cover in a few pages. But I know through my counseling practice that teaching children healthy sexual values and providing correct information about sex is an important part of preventing sexual addiction. As parents, we need to help our children develop a biblically sound, healthy view of sexuality. After all, if we don't teach our children, others will!

It's easy to forget the obvious fact that God created sex in an ideal, pre-fallen world. God declared that it was not good for man to be alone, and so He created a sexual partner for Adam. The intimacy that God wants marriage partners to develop is, in part, expressed through sexual relations that take place within the marriage relationship. Intercourse is to be a pleasurable expression of caring, dynamic intimacy, and respect, not an outlet for emotional passion.

God has allowed sexual relations to continue in a fallen world, and we are responsible to help our children develop healthy understandings of sexuality. Sex education is important. Children need accurate knowledge and information. But it must be shared appropriately and without a sense of shame.

Interestingly, there's no evidence that healthy sex education—telling children the basics of sex and explaining its biblical guidelines—contributes to sexually addictive behavior. In fact, I was surprised that staff workers at the sexual dependency unit at Golden Valley provide a sex education class as part of their routine treatment of sex addicts. The staff has discovered that many sex addicts lack basic factual information about sex, even though they've been involved in sexually addictive behaviors.

Parents unconsciously and naturally communicate sexual attitudes, feelings, and behaviors. Children should see their parents express affection. My sons, for example, see me reach out to my wife and see their mother respond. They know that we enjoy holding hands, kissing, touching, and hugging. Children learn much through observation.

How comfortable are we with our bodies? Do we have healthy or unhealthy attitudes toward sexuality? In a moment of reflection, many of us will recall our parents' attitudes toward sex and the influences they had—good and bad. Did your mother communicate that sex was a burden for her but a man's pleasure? How did your mother respond to your need for your first bra? Was your father embarrassed to talk about wet dreams and discuss your feelings about the girl next door?

Prevention of inaccurate or unhealthy sexual attitudes in children must start with our own attitudes. If we find it difficult and embarrassing to talk about sex, what are we communicating to our children? Is sex embarrassing, something that shouldn't be discussed? Is it wrong to have sexual feelings and desires? When children don't learn about their sexuality in appropriate ways from their parents, they may seek the answers elsewhere—from people who will show and not just tell them. Or they may not talk to anyone about sex and remain in a state of confusion, apprehension, and curiosity toward the opposite sex. Either response may create fertile ground for sexually addictive behaviors.

WARNING SIGNS OF SEXUAL ADDICTION IN OLDER CHILDREN

People often ask me, "How can I tell if my teenager is involved in sexually addictive behavior? And if he or she is, when should I intervene?" Sometimes the parent who asks this already knows that a problem exists.

If a parent finds hard-core porno magazines in a teen's closet, if 900 numbers appear on the phone bill, or if other evidence of possible sexually addictive behavior shows up, it will be difficult to discuss these matters with the child if there has been no healthy pattern of parent-child discussions about important issues. The quality of the parent/child relationship that is necessary to deal with these matters adequately and appropriately should have been built years earlier. That lack of relationship, in part, may have contributed to the child's loneliness and need that led to involvement in sexual fantasy or other behaviors.

Let's assume, however, that the child is curious or experimenting with sexual limits. Let's also assume that the child's behavior isn't well advanced. The child may be using pornography to masturbate, for example, but isn't compulsively masturbating. The teenager may have watched an X-rated film at a friend's house, but doesn't have to watch a film every night. He or she may stare at a scantily dressed girl or boy at the beach and become aroused, but doesn't peep in windows hoping to catch a glimpse of someone naked. If you know or at least strongly suspect that your child is becoming involved in sexual behaviors that go against biblical guidelines, you'd be wise to set aside time to discuss sexual issues together. A few tips may prove helpful here.

Ask nonthreatening questions that touch on important issues. What is your child feeling about sexuality? How are your child's friends dealing with sexual issues? What values and issues of sexuality are significant to your child? How much is your child fantasizing? Masturbating?

Select an opportunity in which communication will be natural and relaxed. This might be at the kitchen table, playing basketball in the driveway, or out on the trail during a backpacking trip.

Don't overreact to behaviors you don't approve of by jumping to the conclusion that your child is headed into a lifetime of compulsive sexual behavior. Responding in anger or panic won't improve communication. Warning a youth, "If you keep doing this, you'll become a sex addict," is a bit like finding a beer can in the back of the car and saying, "Don't you realize if you drink beer you'll become an alcoholic?!" Overreactions stifle communication at a time when there's a real opportunity for your child to talk about deep, important issues.

Encourage communication. The bottom line is whether or not your child feels comfortable with how you're approaching the subject and trusts you enough to express his or her genuine thoughts and feelings. When a sexual temptation arises, your son or daughter may come to you and express questions or concerns about sexual behavior. He or she might say, for example, "This magazine is hard to put down. What does that mean, Dad?" When there is open communication, the child can use you as a resource and know that you won't respond with rejection or punishment.

Recognize when additional help may be needed. Perhaps your efforts to encourage your child to open up won't succeed. Depending on the severity of the behavior and the consequences, you may need professional help. AIDS is spreading through the teenage population, so promiscuity—whether addictive or not—is dangerous as well as immoral. Local Christian counselors, pastors, or other professionals will be able to help you in this counseling decision.

THE CHURCH'S ROLE IN PREVENTION
I'd be remiss if I didn't at least touch on the role that the church can play in the prevention of sexually addictive behaviors. Pastors, Sunday school teachers, and other church leaders who are in regular contact with children and their families have a unique window on how those families operate internally. As such, they often notice a child's sexual difficulties and can intervene.

An example might be a seven-year-old boy who takes extreme interest in young girls in a Sunday school class by touching them inappropriately, asking them to undress, or engaging in "childish" sexual activities. Church leaders may want to learn if this child has been sexually abused.

When there is suspicion of sexual abuse in a Christian home or a child exhibits a sexually addictive behavior, a church representative may be the only person who is aware of the problem. This person should not be fearful of intervention, when triggered by healthy concern and carried out in a loving, sensitive way to find out what's going on.

In some states, the representative must also report the situation to the local child protection services.

When children demonstrate sexual difficulties or seem incapable of initiating and maintaining relationships with others, church workers need to read literature on sexual abuse and be prepared to ask the child and the parent(s) important questions. It takes time to develop a relationship with a young child or adolescent, to reach the point at which the child will speak openly about sexuality. But I'm convinced that there's an enormous opportunity for the church to intervene in deeply troubled families raising kids who will experience extreme problems in the next generation unless family crises are resolved.

All things being equal, parents who are willing to evaluate themselves and their relationship with God and who seek to develop appropriate intimate relationships with their children probably have the least to worry about in the area of potential sexual addiction. Parents who should be worrying about sexual addiction in their families will likely not even read a book such as this.

There are no guarantees that our children will not become sex addicts, even if we "do everything right." That in itself should move us toward greater dependence on God.

CHAPTER

✦ 7 ✦

Sexual Addiction in the Church

R obert appeared to be succeeding in his calling. Upon entering seminary, his motivation was to serve God, to give of himself through teaching the Word of God, to care for the Lord's flock, and to devote himself to prayer and Bible study.

But Robert's inner life was dark and murky.

In high school, Robert had been attracted to one of the more popular girls. To his amazement, she had talked with him in the hallway and seemed to enjoy his company. So he finally got up the nerve to ask her for a date and was thrilled when she said yes.

As the special Friday approached, he couldn't concentrate on anything besides the time they'd have. His mind wandered to the romantic setting in which he'd touch her soft, smooth hand and see the tender response in her eyes. This moment would fulfill the craving that had gone unmet for so long.

Finally the moment arrived. Robert drove to the girl's home, his heart pounding with anticipation. When her mother answered the door, the confused look on her face turned Robert's blood cold. "My daughter has already left with another young man."

Waves of disbelief, fear, and shame washed over Robert. He wanted to become invisible, to run away, to turn back the clock and erase his trip to that door. During the sleepless nights that followed, he resolved never to be burned again, never to allow such pain, rejection, and shame into his life.

Eventually, Robert dated other girls who weren't as popular but ended each relationship after several dates. He also began using pornography and sexual fantasy to relieve his pain.

During college, Robert accepted Christ. His Christian devotion, ability to speak, and leadership qualities brought him recognition, praise, and a sense of purpose. In his senior year he met Mary, a woman who appreciated him, affirmed his Christian commitment, and found security in him. A month after they started dating they became sexually involved. Two months later they were engaged. After graduation they married, and almost immediately Mary began to lose her desire for sexual relations.

The next few years, while Robert was attending seminary, were financially and relationally stressful. Only one among many peers preparing for ministry, Robert was an average student. Needing to feel good, he began visiting the local porno bookstore and watching live nude dancing in private booths.

After seminary, Robert succeeded in his role as a pastor. His churches grew, but so did his stress and isolation. He faced acute loneliness and deep fears of abandonment and rejection because of his sexual addiction. These fears caused him to withdraw from others, which further increased his loneliness. As part of his ministry of counseling, he met privately with women in the church who deeply admired and trusted him. During these sessions, they shared the deepest, most intimate parts of their lives and seemed to be more accepting of him than Mary was.

Audrey, who had been married for three years to an abusive husband, found security in Robert's warm, sensitive, caring nature. As counseling continued, Robert's mind became preoccupied with her. Prompted by her most intimate disclosures, all his emotions, dreams, and fantasies became embodied in the woman sitting with him who tearfully shared the pain and humiliation of her husband's abuse. One evening he moved out of his chair to embrace her, and both were instantly intoxicated with the warmth of each other's body and the thought of erotic contact. His ministry, the families who would be affected, and even his relationship with God seemed less important to him than the promise of their secret intimacy.

That night Robert crossed a primary boundary that led him to have endless affairs with other women and to hire prostitutes. His ability to bring each church he pastored to a new level of growth became both an opportunity for new affairs and a way to avoid discovery.

In recent years the church has been rudely reminded of a basic tenet: Christian leaders are not immune to sexual sin. The impact of the immoral behavior of people in key ministry positions can't be measured. I believe these well-known leaders who have fallen are but the tip of the iceberg and that the problem of sexual addiction is widespread within the church.

Consider, for instance, the results of a *Leadership Magazine* survey. Of the 300 pastors who responded, 23 percent indicated that they had done something sexual with someone other than their spouse. Twelve percent reported having intercourse with someone other than their spouse, and 61 percent admitted to fantasizing occasionally about having sex with someone other than their spouse. Twenty-five percent indicated that they sexually fantasized weekly or even daily.[1]

These statistics don't reveal whether the pastors were sexually addicted or were just committing illicit sexual acts. But the evidence indicates that problems with sexual sin are rampant within the church, and more situations are sure to surface as more states enact laws against sexual exploitation and sexual violation of professional trust. The number of Christian people who call me for sexual addiction counseling is increasing, which is true of other Christian colleagues I talk with regularly.

For fourteen years I've been ministering to sex addicts, many of whom are Christian clergymen. Statistics about sex addiction in the church can't capture the hardness of heart that enables a pastor to believe in God's truth and simultaneously fondle a prostitute or a member of his congregation. I hope I never get used to seeing the stark barrenness of a man called to shepherd the flock of God who is void of integrity and lost in the hollowness of sexual fantasy and fear.

Statistics don't begin to capture the countless, agonizing stories of the victims of sexual addiction in the church: wives betrayed by their husbands, husbands betrayed by their wives, congregations paralyzed by scandal, careers ruined, marriages and families destroyed, and the image of Christians smeared.

Don, a youth pastor, was arrested for sexual molestation of four preteen girls in his program. Stan, a former minister of music, was dismissed because he repeatedly visited a gay bar. Frank, married for three years and soon to become a father, was arrested for soliciting a prostitute. Bill had to face his elders when they learned he'd had affairs with three different counselees. Mark, a respected elder, was asked to resign when the husband of the woman with whom he'd had an eight-year-long affair discovered the adultery. A brilliant and popular professor at a Christian college lost his position when several students reported being sexually involved with him. Robert, a leader of a boy's program at his church, was arrested for sexually molesting two boys. A respected writer and speaker, Janet had an affair and left her family. Lois, a single woman in her mid-forties who served as the dean of women at a Christian college for twenty years, quietly resigned amid allegations that she'd had lesbian relationships with students. Phyllis and Carol, a popular ministry team, ended their ministry after stories that they were lovers began to surface.

Isolated incidents? Hardly. I'm sure many of us have heard of someone within our respective Christian communities who has committed sexual misconduct. One church in my community has faced the murder of a beloved woman by her husband's lover. Last week a pastor called me from Arizona to say that he's a sex addict and needs treatment. This week I'm counseling a pastor who has been involved with prostitutes on a weekly basis for the past ten years.

Why Is Sexual Addiction So Prevalent in the Church?
Throughout the Bible, God sets forth clear guidelines for our sexual behavior. He commands us to reserve sex for marriage and not to have sex with relatives, animals, or people of the same sex. He tells us that we are to flee sexual immorality, that our bodies are His temple, and that we're not to pollute our minds with lustful thoughts.[2]

Yet Christians continue to break His laws regarding sexual behavior, and the church often appears unable to deal with sexual sins. Why are so many Christians sexually addicted or committing sexual sins? Is it because Christian parents fail to raise their children correctly?

Is it a renewed level of spiritual warfare, with Satan exploiting our weaknesses? Is it a lack of commitment to Christian principles, the breakup and breakdown of the family unit? Does the fault lie in poor self-esteem, fear of rejection, or being raised in shame-based families?

As I speak at conferences and in other ways interact with Christian lay people and leaders about sexual addiction, I typically find them to be confused, disoriented, and groping in the dark for solutions to sexual addiction. I believe several factors have clearly led to the rise of sexual addiction within the church.

Spiritual Conformity

I've often reflected on what I experienced growing up in the church. A variety of preachers challenged me to do what was right, but I felt condemned because I couldn't quite meet their standards. I couldn't understand why everyone around me seemed to live better Christian lives than I did. What I didn't understand then was that many of them weren't really living more godly lives; they just appeared to be!

As a result, my response to the challenge of godly living was to try harder. I prayed more, witnessed more, read more Scripture, became active in more Christian activities, and did more of anything that was considered "the right thing to do." My efforts did result in my doing more of what I should have been doing, and less of what I shouldn't have been doing. However, I was motivated to conform to others' expectations and perceptions rather than to develop a genuine, passionate heart for God. I was determined to improve, if it cost me everything, so I'd look great on the outside. Eventually I had to face the fact that my commitment to obedience was really just an attempt to make my life fulfilling and mold it into what I wanted it to be.

It took me years to understand that my spiritual motivations were wrong. The point hit home as I struggled to do well in a college math class. Concerned that I'd fail the class, lose my student draft deferment, and end up in Vietnam, I went to talk to my advisor. A mature, seasoned Christian, he listened as my questions poured out. "Why am I struggling with this course when I'm so committed to the Lord to use my education for ministry? I've committed my life to full-time Christian service, so why aren't things going well?" What I was really asking, in my heart, is this: *Doesn't my good life obligate God to help me overcome my weakness in math?*

My advisor's response confused me by countering my understanding of how the Christian life works. "Obeying God," he said, "is not a formula for God to provide you with everything you consider to be essential to your life."

I left his office a bit puzzled, thinking that he either knew more about God than I had considered or that age had somehow distorted his thinking. Basically I ignored his words and continued to obey God because of what I thought He would do for me.

But ten years later, my question returned to shake my carefully built foundations when our daughter died shortly after birth.

During that time of grief, if you had asked me to define God's goodness, I would have told you I had no idea what it meant. If you had pressed me, I might have added, "I only know He exists, and I believe that Jesus is the Son of God. But beyond those points I'm bewildered." I struggled back to a stronger faith but remained confused about the meaning of God's goodness and wondered if it had anything to do with obedience.

I hadn't realized that my obedience to God was based more on a fear of pain and difficulty than on a spiritual passion to know and follow Him out of joyful desire. In *Inside Out*, Dr. Larry Crabb wrote of this issue: "Too often, a commitment to obedience reflects not a passionate desire to pursue God, but a stubbornly fearful determination to not feel deep frustration and personal pain."[3]

Years later, a godly counselor asked me the toughest, most penetrating questions I've ever been asked and told me I was a "weak man." His love, the boldest I'd ever experienced, caused me to look at myself, my relationships with others, and — most crucially — my relationship with God. A process began that still continues in my life today. I can now say, without question, "God is good!" I have tasted His goodness, which in fact is often the sweetest during unresolved difficulties.

Al was a fifty-two-year-old pastor from the West Coast. As a boy, he had never felt his father's strong confidence in him. As a teenager and young man, he had faithfully attended all church activities and striven to live an obedient Christian life. He fell in love with Denise, a wonderful Christian woman he felt would give him all he ever wanted—in a wife, companion, and friend. During their courtship they carefully avoided sexual intimacy, desiring to remain pure until marriage.

As their courtship progressed, Al went to college for a semester, but they wrote many letters and talked frequently on the phone. During Christmas break, Al returned home, eager to see Denise. One evening she insisted on making love with him at her parents' home. Al easily gave in to her demands, but he felt deep guilt and shame for failing to live up to his Christian standards.

Several days later, deeply troubled, he shared his guilt with Denise, who stated, "I don't really love you. I've been seeing another guy and think I'm pregnant. So I wanted to make love to you because the other guy would never be pressured into marrying me."

Crushed and enraged, Al returned to college, married a different woman, and entered the ministry. Outwardly the track of his life seemed to be intact. He sought to serve the Lord obediently. His life was a model of Christian devotion. He had a respectable Christian marriage and well-mannered children. But the inside track of his life was ugly.

When Al had returned to college after that Christmas with Denise, his relationship with women had changed. In his mind he now knew what life, relationships, and women were about: sex. He viewed each woman as a physical experience in which he'd be in control and not be hurt. Women were to be used for pleasure, nothing more.

When Al found seventeen-year-old Sally, who was willing to be "molded according to his exact wishes" and wanted a husband who would manage her life so she could be happy, he married her. It seemed like a perfect match. Each provided what the other wanted—safety and security—and each was willing to enter the conspiracy of being what the other wanted.

But Al continued to indulge in sexual sin. He had physical contact with a series of women, went to peep shows, and masturbated two to three times a day when he felt his ministry was most successful. "I justified my behavior," he told me later, "because my sexual contacts with the other women never involved intercourse."

❖   ❖   ❖

Like Al, and like me, many Christians have tried to do all the right things for the wrong reasons. They have tried to impress themselves, God, and others by demonstrating that they could successfully conform to the expectations of other Christians and live good lives. Because of their emphasis on conformity, they haven't always built a strong spiritual foundation.

Consequently, these Christians have left themselves vulnerable to sexual temptation and ensuing sexually addictive behaviors. Instead of depending on God with a spirit of perseverance and endurance in the face of disappointment, they have tried to find fulfillment and avoid pain on their own through behavioral conformity. Instead of focusing on the sinfulness of their hearts, they have focused on looking good to others.

Externalism

Closely related to conformity, *externalism* results when we move toward the safety of measuring ourselves and others by what we can observe on the outside.

It's easy to persist in believing that observable or measurable factors in human behavior are appropriate criteria in determining people's character. For instance, "holiness" is often defined by what Christians do or don't do—how they adhere to certain standards of living that are considered godly. If a person dresses with a better label, has a dignified position, drives a nice automobile, speaks eloquently, and is faithful in all Christian duties, it's easy to think this person has developed character and maturity. God recognized this tendency and said, "The LORD does not look at the things man looks at. Man looks at the outward appearance, but the LORD looks at the heart" (1 Samuel 16:7).

Of course there's no question that godly people shouldn't do certain things. The Bible gives us God's standards, which are to be consistent with who we are as followers of Christ. The problem is, when we place too much emphasis on our external behaviors it's easy to avoid considering our hearts—the core of our being and the origin of our motivations, goals, and desires.

Jesus gave His strongest recorded rebuke to the religious leaders of His day who placed far too much emphasis on external behaviors and neglected their inner spiritual development:

"Woe to you, teachers of the law and Pharisees, you hypocrites! You clean the outside of the cup and dish, but inside they are full of greed and self-indulgence. Blind Pharisee! First clean the inside of the cup and dish, and then the outside also will be clean.

"Woe to you, teachers of the law and Pharisees, you hypocrites! You are like whitewashed tombs, which look beautiful on the outside but on the inside are full of dead men's bones and everything unclean. In the same way, on the outside you appear to people as righteous but on the inside you are full of hypocrisy and wickedness." (Matthew 23:25-28)

Quite often what a person says and does on the outside, publicly, is in dramatic contrast to what he or she is like on the inside. Countless people have been dangerously confused when a person of respect, particularly a member of the clergy, is found to be leading a double life.

I can still remember the day my father told me that a youth minister I highly respected and who had greatly influenced my life spiritually had been removed from ministry because several young boys had accused him of sexual molestation. I was shocked. *How could this be?* I thought. *He was so godly!* As it turned out, he had appeared to be everything a youth minister should be, but he had neglected his inner walk with God and failed to deal with the sin in his heart.

A successful pastor told me his shameful story, which included getting his secretary pregnant, going to bars to see nude dancers, pornography, a fetish for women's soiled underwear, and being arrested for sexually grabbing a woman on the street. Until his arrest, his public life—his ministry, preaching, spiritual image—appeared to be above reproach. I asked him how his church members were responding to the allegations and arrest. "They don't believe the newspapers," he told me. "They think I'm being framed." We so easily believe what we can see and observe, rather than engaging in the hard work of looking below the surface.

As a counselor whose ministry focuses on Christian leaders and ministers who struggle with sexual addiction, I'm not surprised anymore when situations like this arise. My shock at such revelations has been replaced with deep sorrow over the deceptiveness and depth of sin in the human heart. As I look at my own life, I see how easy it is to look good, to be a superb externalist rather than confessing my sinful desires and striving to know God.

Superficial, external obedience to Christian standards that lacks the passionate pursuit of the person of Christ is a symptom of blatant avoidance of sin in the heart. I can't prove it statistically, but I have a strong suspicion that the sexual misconduct that is rampant in the church today is connected to the propensity of men and women to neglect the cleaning of the inside of the cup and dish. Jesus declared that the foulness of sin comes from an impure heart, not from the violation of external rules:

> "What comes out of a man is what makes him 'unclean.' For
> from within, out of men's hearts, come evil thoughts, sexual
> immorality, theft, murder, adultery, greed, malice, deceit, lewd-
> ness, envy, slander, arrogance and folly. All these evils come
> from inside and make a man 'unclean.'" (Mark 7:20-23)

Charles Spurgeon, the noted evangelist and writer, said of this passage, "[Jesus] draws up a diagnosis of the disease with fearless truthfulness, . . . that religion is not a matter of observation or non-observation of washings and outward rites; but that the whole matter is spiritual, and has to do with man's inmost self, with the understanding, the will, the emotions, the conscience, and all else which makes up the heart of man."[4] Simply living by the rules, obeying, and doing what is right, doesn't indicate a pure heart. Until we deal with our internal uncleanness, we shouldn't be shocked at sexual misconduct within the church.

Desire for Easy Solutions

We all experience difficult circumstances, from the mundane to the excruciating. We naturally want relief from the pain, and so we naturally gravitate toward a commitment not to be hurt again. This commitment, however, significantly influences our view of God. If we're not careful, we tenaciously pursue freedom from pain and wallow in the deceptiveness of our ability to reconstruct God and His reality according to our desires. Deceived into thinking that we can control further damage to ourselves, we may move through life by paying lip service to God with correct theology while at the same time raising our fists in protest to our Creator.

Often within the church we look for convenient methods, formulas, or structures that will help us manage difficult problems. When marriages fall apart, we want to know what to do. When kids turn to drugs, we want a plan of action. When debt threatens to overwhelm us, we look for a method of recovery and debt consolidation. When we or someone we love begins to struggle with sexual addiction and experience its painful consequences, we want methods, guidelines, principles, or plans that will lead us out of the darkness and agony. *There must be a way out of this,* we think. *Someone must know what will work. If I could just find it, there'd be hope. If I could just manage things, I could handle the addiction. I'd be released from emptiness, confusion, and compulsion.*

Notice, though, that this hope is based on finding solutions — the right plans, principles, and structures — rather than on grappling with the issues of sin and repentance. It falsely assumes that the problems we face in life are the *real* problems. It discounts or ignores spiritual issues by assuming that God's deliverance, healing, and provision will free us from the difficult circumstances of life that so often beset us. Consequently we search for the right plans and principles to guide us.

Consider the popularity of twelve-step recovery groups, which offer a structure for recovery, a way to manage the painful issues that we recognize need to be addressed. There's no question that many issues surfacing in recovery groups need to be faced. However, my concern is that many people involved in twelve-step recovery groups primarily focus on improving their quality of living rather than on the deeper issue of knowing and serving God.

When we concentrate on recovery from a destructive behavior rather than on how God can regenerate our inner being and enable us to cope with suffering, it's easy to operate on the assumption that our hearts are naturally good. But we need more than a process of restructuring our lives. We need to receive the supernatural work of the Spirit of God and the renewal of our sinful hearts by grace.

Our Self-Centered Expectations of God

One question it's difficult to get people to answer honestly is, "What has God really promised to do in your life?" It's difficult because people often initially answer this question based on improvements they'd like to see in their lives: a better marriage, a better job, better health. After all, they reason, isn't that the abundant life?

When we begin to believe that God's plan for our lives is to improve our relationships and circumstances *now*, churches quickly fill with people who focus on the primacy of personal need, evaluate God's goodness in terms of meeting those needs, and subtly move to justify anything that feels like it's from God.

The passion for the abundant life, however we define it, can become greater than a passion for the Lord. That shift is subtle but humanistic if our real goal is easing our pain, meeting our needs, and speeding up our recovery without basing our actions on a desire to love and worship God.

Our fallen hearts do not naturally believe that God is good and can be trusted with our deep desires. So we may subtly redefine God and justify forms of living that demonstrate our need to direct our own lives. *Doesn't God want us to be happy?* some Christians reason. *He couldn't possibly want us to be deprived of enjoying life.* Satan tempted Eve by questioning God's goodness and implying that God's directive not to eat of the fruit was a hindrance to having more of life. This was a subtle, seemingly innocent appeal to self-interest, care of oneself, and the implied right to pursue what seems necessary for well-being.

One sex addict involved in an affair and unsure of his commitment to his wife said to me, "When I'm with her [the other woman], I feel so alive. How could anything so good be so wrong?" Self-justification comes easily when we start with our needs and define God as the resource who will meet those needs. It's easy to view God as the One who heals those needs rather than the One who deals with the sin that leads to eternal, spiritual death. It's easy to say that the hope of God improving our lives is what sustains us rather than taking the biblical position that the hope of eternal glory makes our suffering bearable.

If we turn to God and don't receive "deliverance" from our difficulties, we often choose one of two options. We may try to increase our faith to motivate Him to reward us with an answer to our prayers. Or we may increase our efforts and argue the fairness of our case. Notice that in doing so we define God's goodness by His response to what we believe to be essential to our well-being. By implication, we consider God to be negligent — or at best, guilty of mismanagement.

C. S. Lewis, writing about his struggles with the death of his wife and the issue of God's goodness, spoke of God as the "Cosmic Sadist" and the "Great Vivisector."[5] But Lewis realized, as we all should, that we can't judge God's goodness by how He responds, intervenes, changes, or improves the circumstances of our lives.

Jesus stated clearly, "In this world you will have trouble. But take heart! I have overcome the world" (John 16:33). Paul also challenged us: "If only for this life we have hope in Christ, we are to be pitied more than all men" (1 Corinthians 15:19). God's primary purpose is not to offset the pain of living in this sinful world. He doesn't exist simply to solve each and every problem we face in life—or even the ones we perceive will crush us. He calls us to become absorbed in fulfilling His will and purpose, to deny ourselves for the good of others and to His glory. Our joy should be in serving and loving God.

Light Regard for "Evil Thoughts"

Perhaps because none of us can know the thoughts of another, the church often de-emphasizes the relationship of thought life to behavior. It's easier to react to evil acts than to address the types of thoughts we should have. It's easy to assume that thoughts don't matter as much as actions.

C. H. Spurgeon thought differently. "Thoughts," he wrote, "are the eggs of words and actions, and within the thoughts lie compacted and condensed all the villainy of actual transgressions."[6]

What begins within the mind originates from the depths of our sinful hearts. Evil thoughts, once pondered, stimulate the desires of our soul, and ultimately the lust that is followed by action. The source of the action lies within the heart. James wrote, "Each one is tempted when, by his own evil desire, he is dragged away and enticed. Then, after desire has conceived, it gives birth to sin; and sin, when it is full-grown, gives birth to death" (James 1:14-15).

As Christians, we can't afford to neglect our minds, to allow sinful thoughts to run rampant. Paul wrote, "Do not conform any longer to the pattern of this world, but be transformed by the renewing of your mind. Then you will be able to test and approve what God's will is—his good, pleasing and perfect will" (Romans 12:2).

Again, in Philippians 4:8, Paul emphasized the importance of dwelling on the right things in our minds: "Whatever is true, whatever is noble, whatever is right, whatever is pure, whatever is lovely, whatever is admirable—if anything is excellent or praiseworthy—think about such things."

God knows our thoughts and judges us accordingly. "O LORD, you have searched me and you know me," David wrote. "Search me, O God, and know my heart; test me and know my anxious thoughts" (Psalm 139:1,23). It's important that we examine our thoughts and commit them to God.

Toleration of Sexual Sin

I'm keenly struck by the number of church leaders and lay people who tolerate sexual sin in their midst. Rather than confronting a person whose sexual behavior is not biblical, Christians often look the other way. This occurs most frequently when the person who is committing the sexual sin is not in a high-profile position. It's as if sexual sin within the congregation is considered okay if it doesn't get out of control or in some way bring blatant hurt or shame to other members.

When sexual sin is discovered, quite often church leaders fall for the sex addict's rationalizations: "I know what I'm doing is wrong; I'm trying to stop." "I've discussed it with a counselor and am working on it." "I'm sorry. I just need more time to get things straight in my own mind."

Paul, on the other hand, said, "Among you there must not be even a hint of sexual immorality, or of any kind of impurity" (Ephesians 5:3). Failure to deal with even the hint of sexual sin has resulted in untold shattered lives and congregations.

Lack of Commitment to Restoration Among Believers

Godly men and women are to be busy in the work of personal restoration: "Brothers, if someone is caught in a sin, you who are spiritual should restore him gently" (Galatians 6:1). The Apostle Paul directs us toward a process of setting things right.

Interestingly, Paul isn't focusing on acts of sin in this admonition. He emphasizes that mature Christians are to move into the lives of people who wander from God's laws and are to help correct their self-dependence. In a spirit of meekness, mature Christians are to help people recognize that they have sinned, to encourage them to confess their sins, and to join with them as they return to godly living.

It's not easy to actively restore others to fellowship with God. It's easier to let people "do their own thing." It's also easy to delude ourselves into thinking that we're objective enough to recognize and correct our faults—to restore ourselves to wholeness.

The truth is that *all of us need others who love us enough to confront us honestly and tell us when we're wrong or going in the wrong direction.* Solomon wrote of the impact that loving confrontation should have:

> He who listens to a life-giving rebuke
> will be at home among the wise.
> He who ignores discipline despises himself,
> but whoever heeds correction gains understanding.
> (Proverbs 15:31-32)

Unfortunately, many of us don't know others well enough to have "earned the right to speak." We're so busy in our own worlds of business and family, schedules and reschedules that we hardly have time to figure out where we're heading next, much less care about the spiritual direction of someone else.

Recently some churches have begun to realize the power of godly restoration. Home groups are being formed in which members meet regularly to deal with tough issues. Sunday school classes are becoming times of discussion as well as teaching. But the church has a long way to go in fostering true, concerned restoration among its members.

OBSTACLES THAT BLOCK THE CHURCH'S UNDERSTANDING OF SEXUAL ADDICTION

Right now, the church must face a number of obstacles that block its understanding of sexual addiction and thereby limit its ability to offer healing restoration to sex addicts.

Fear of Sexual Addiction

Many pastors and counselors don't recognize the warning signs of developing addiction and, believing that only experts can help sex addicts, are afraid to become involved. It is true that sexual addiction appears, at times, to defy limited understanding. Even clinically trained, professional counselors are sometimes reluctant to counsel sex addicts. However, although there's no doubt that sex addicts require competent counseling, there's a danger in viewing sexual addiction as an unusual problem that can be handled only by an "expert."

Sexual addiction has many complicated facets, but godly people who aren't experts in sexual addiction can reach out to help a sex addict and discuss issues of the heart. By being afraid of or unwilling to deal with sex addicts, pastors and counselors have not done as much as they could to help Christians who struggle with sexual addiction experience God's healing and restoration.

Many Christians are also afraid to discuss sex and sexual addiction. When the topic comes up, three responses are common. First, there's a voyeuristic curiosity, a stirring of our deepest cravings for the forbidden and the possibility of feeding our own fantasies. In blunt terms, we are curious about how someone else does it—at least to feed our minds if not influence our behaviors. Perhaps we even wish, deep inside, that we had tried such behaviors before we got married or became Christians.

Second, sexual addiction is a troubling and threatening topic. Its very mention often produces an intense, internal discomfort that is frequently manifested by averting the eyes, lowering the head, moving into another room, or grinning uncomfortably. Some people inject humor into the situation in an attempt to diminish the moment's intensity; others make every effort to remain calm, not wanting to give even a hint of discomfort or fear.

Third, we may fear that if we talk about sex—and our feelings and thoughts—others will know us for who we are, that our lustful thoughts, fantasies, and passions will be exposed. The hint that we engage in sexual fantasy (which might imply we have a revolting perversion) brings terror to our bones.

Are these simply reactions to sexual addictions or indications of spiritual weakness? On the outside, we can proficiently maintain the impression of respectability and spiritual maturity. Inside, however, may lie the hidden reality of sordid thoughts and rank passions. To some people, just reading about sexual addiction may arouse hidden fears of exposure. *Will the slip of my tongue or these words on the page,* they may wonder, *drag me into seeing myself and my wretchedness? Will exploring a biblical understanding of sexual addiction draw me into a vortex so powerful that it will lead me away from God and into darkness? Will it cause me to face the darkness of sin in my own heart?*

Addressing the problem of sexual addiction forces us to go to the very core of who we are as fallen creatures, to grapple with the wickedness of our desire to control life and relationships and our determination to use false intimacy to escape our woundedness. We must recognize that it's a small step indeed from having an intact life externally that lacks spiritual depth to becoming involved in sexually addictive behaviors. None of us is immune to sexual sin.

The View that Sexual Sin Is a "Worse" Sin

If I were to gather a number of Christian people together to make a list of the "worst sins," no doubt sexual sin would be right near the top. There are many possible explanations for this, but the fact is that such a perspective isn't biblical. Sin is sin. When we sin, we sin against the Holy God and His laws. When we gossip, we sin. When we lust, we sin. Of course some sins have greater consequences than other sins. But that's not the issue. In God's eyes, all sins are the same and must be confessed.

When sexual sin achieves notoriety over other sins, several things occur. The strongly forbidden appears more tempting. The person who sins sexually is viewed in a far harsher light than the one who gossips, which causes a sex addict to want to hide even deeper in the safe burrow of fantasy and isolation. So it's no wonder that some sex addicts choose to avoid confession and carry their pain alone.

Simplistic Views of Sexual Addiction

As Christians become aware of a person's sexual addiction, they sometimes view sexual addiction as simply a failure to live up to Christian standards. Using exhortation and discipline, they respond moralistically and use biblical truths in damaging ways. "Just turn to God. Live up to His standards. Change your behavior now." "Why don't you live a godly life?" "You're a moral failure; shape up and act the way God wants you to act." "Why do you do those awful things?" "You're a pervert."

Quite often, a person wrestling with sexual sin hears comments like these from well-meaning but misguided Christians who haven't yet learned about the depth of their own sin and the complexities of sexual addiction. People who make these types of judgments (verbally or mentally) view sexual addiction as a yielding of the flesh to perversion and think that rebuke and exhortation are the cure.

Occasionally this type of rebuke seems to work. The sex addict works hard to stop his or her behaviors (but usually just gets better at hiding them). But the elusive deceitfulness of the addict's heart that energizes his or her desires is ignored. Even worse, self-righteous judgments both overlook and put salt into the sex addict's deep hurts, thus driving him or her away from God rather than toward His mercy and love.

Simply exhorting the sex addict to quit doing addictive behaviors is a bit like prescribing strenuous exercise and a good diet to someone who complains of chest pains. The source of the pain is correctly diagnosed, but the treatment is reckless, given the seriousness of the underlying problem.

Remember the story in John 8 about the woman caught in the act of adultery? The pious leaders criticized her for her behavior and dragged her in front of Jesus. Jesus didn't say, "Lady, why did you do that horrible act? Stop doing those kinds of things this moment because what you're doing is wrong!" No, He recognized that sin caused her problem and that no rebuke could change that. He dispersed the crowd by inviting anyone without sin to cast the first stone at her and then urged her to "leave your life of sin."

Sex addicts can't change their behaviors without help from God and wise counsel. None of us can find adequate relational satisfaction or sufficient relief from relational pain without help. To expect something different from the sex addict is to heap more shame on the addict and encourage Christians to respond to tough relational issues with simplistic solutions.

Yes, God has given us laws to obey. Yes, He calls us to be holy and to represent Him in a hurting world. But He deals with us gently, too. He knows our weaknesses and offers His help. He didn't rebuke the Samaritan woman at the well for her many sexual encounters with men. In fact, mostly He asked questions, listened, and showed a love that shook her life and the lives of others in her community.

Much in our culture teaches us that we are powerful and strong, able to fulfill the American dream and move from a log cabin to the White House. We learn that if we work hard, we'll be rewarded with prestige, a loving family, and material blessings. We learn that we can make it if we just try harder and believe that those who haven't made it didn't try hard enough. But believing in ourselves and the fruit of our efforts works against the fact that we are sinful and can escape sinful behaviors only with God's help.

Viewing Sexual Addiction as a Disease

Because I already addressed this topic in chapter 3, I won't cover it thoroughly here. But it's important for us to recognize several related points that have blocked our understanding of sexual addiction.

First, *sexual addiction is not a disease over which the sex addict has no control.* Sex addicts make significant choices and must be held accountable for those choices. Also, treating sexual addiction as a disease easily leads us to treat the sex addict's behaviors instead of the sin that causes the behaviors.

Only God can help a person overcome sin. Treatment programs can influence a person to stop committing certain sexual acts, but the programs can't address the root cause of those behaviors without bringing the power of Christ to bear on the issues of the heart.

Denial of Sexual Addiction

The church system itself puts pressure on us to deny spiritual crises. It goes against our values to mistrust Christian people—pastors, elders, lay people—so it's easy to overlook or even ignore their sexually addictive behaviors.

Although established by God and set apart from the secular world, the church nevertheless is a community of people who have problems, who face tough issues, who are tempted, and who fall. Failing to recognize the existence of sexual addiction and take preventive steps allows sexual sin to gain a deeper foothold in people's lives and in the church as a whole. God hates sin. He will forgive those who come to Him in repentance, but He will cast away those who refuse to confess their sins and deny their sinfulness (see 1 Thessalonians 4:3-8, Hebrews 10:26-31).

Certainly it's not easy to accept the reality of sexual addiction in Christian churches. It's even harder to accept that someone we know and love is a sex addict. Dealing with sexual addiction moves us closer to the dark pit of our own sinfulness, for we must face the fact that no one is immune to the allure of false intimacy as a way out of dealing with the pain and hurt we all face in relationships. But we must dare to face ourselves and our pain in order to truly respond in love to the sex addict who desperately needs restoration.

Viewing Sexual Addiction as Demonic

Friends and relatives of sex addicts often find addicts' behavior to be out of character with their good qualities and their Christian values. So there's a tendency to think, *This behavior must be the result of demonic activity.*

There's no doubt that "our struggle is not against flesh and blood, but against the rulers, against the authorities, against the powers of this dark world and against the spiritual forces of evil in the heavenly realms" (Ephesians 6:12). Satan uses all manner of temptations, including sexual ones, to lead God's people into sin. However, some church leaders and lay people immediately conclude that sexual addiction is caused by demons and react in extreme ways. Either they try, through prayer, to "drive out the sexual demons" or they are afraid to deal with the sex addict's problems.

Prayer is a dynamic power that can make a difference in a sex addict's life, but counseling is also needed. Satanic activity can influence a sex addict's behaviors, but so can many other factors. Again, the church must be careful not to create formula approaches to sexual addiction. Doing so can lead to more extensive problems when, for example, a sex addict who has been prayed for and "delivered" realizes that his or her sexual compulsions still exist. Simply treating sexual addiction as demonic activity also fails to address the root cause of sin in the addict's heart.

In the next chapter, we'll explore how the church can deal positively with sexual addiction. We'll look at the church's ministry of healing in sex addicts' lives and show the positive changes that can take place when the church responds firmly and lovingly to confront and restore sex addicts to a renewed relationship with God and the Body of Christ.

CHAPTER

❖ 8 ❖

The Church
as a Healing Community

S taring at his desk behind the closed door of his study, Tom felt the pain weighing him down. In front of him lay the letter of resignation. *Why?* Tom kept asking himself. *Why did this happen?*

Bill, a faithful elder with a fine wife and three small children, had handed him the letter less than an hour earlier. Their ensuing discussion had revealed that Bill had had a five-year affair with a married woman in the congregation who was a Sunday school teacher. Bill had also revealed that he frequently masturbated, purchased a lot of pornographic material, and occasionally visited topless bars.

What do I do now? Tom wondered. *I have to do something, but what? What will happen to the families involved, to the children? How will other people respond?*

❖   ❖   ❖

Perhaps you have been in Tom's situation and know the paralyzing emotions that threaten to overwhelm you as you sift through the options. As a pastor, elder, or other church member, how do you deal with such a crisis? How do you respond to sexual behavior that is immoral, destructive, and out of control? How do you handle

167

the devastating consequences to wives, husbands, children, relatives, friends, and congregation?

Unfortunately, there are no easy answers or pat formulas for this situation. If you're reading this chapter to discover an easy solution, please read the rest of the book first! Pray for wisdom and for a soft, loving heart that will remain strong in the face of evil but tenderly long for the sex addict to be restored. Most of all, make sure that as you move into an addict's life you are prepared to deal with the core issues of his or her heart.

BIBLICAL SELF-EXAMINATION

Obviously, each person caught in the bonds of sexual addiction needs spiritual renewal. To undertake a ministry of healing in someone's life requires firm leadership. Churches often identify a professional counselor as the primary resource when a problem as complex as sexual addiction surfaces. Such a counselor can play a key role, but the most basic requirement of the person who ministers to the sex addict has less to do with education, credentials, or even experience than with spiritual qualifications. This is because if the problem of sexual addiction is an evidence of spiritual adultery—as I believe it is—then the sex addict needs to receive healing with help from someone who is spiritual, who pursues God with all of his or her being. Paul states, "If someone is caught in a sin, you who are spiritual should restore him gently" (Galatians 6:1).

The question of which spiritual leader(s) should be involved in the healing process, then, is primarily one of spiritual maturity. Spiritual qualification is an issue of personal self-examination, not of licenses or degrees. Years of Bible training, years of being a Christian, or even years spent in Christian leadership are not the measure of spiritual maturity. Most important is a heart that is full of passion for God.

We cannot presume that those who seem to be the most likely candidates to undertake the ministry of healing don't struggle with the same secret sins. For instance, one Christian leader who was involved with pornography, 900 numbers, and topless bars told me, "My ministry was heard by thousands of radio listeners, but I haven't prayed for years and don't care about reading my Bible." Thus, anyone preparing for a ministry of healing must examine his or her own heart and determine the direction it pursues to find satisfaction and relief from pain.

In many ways, living a ministry of healing is the opposite of living a life of sexual addiction. The person involved in healing lives in order to give himself or herself in love for the sake of others; the sex addict takes whatever can be obtained for the sake of self.

All of us, on some level, have damaged others by being more committed to ourselves than to others. All of us have found satisfaction in false gods. Although we might not have been involved in sexual addiction, our styles of relating to people in some degree of false intimacy and self-protection are evidence of our lack of love. The following questions can help each of us examine the motives of our hearts:

- How do I manage the emptiness I feel in this fallen world?
- Am I committed to finding relief when I demand it, or do I eagerly anticipate life in eternity and groan at the difference between this fallen world and life as God created it to be?
- Do I refuse to accept the fact that I'm a stranger in this fallen world? Do I use my Christian walk to obtain something for myself and gain self-fulfillment?
- Have I grieved over my own sinful heart?
- Have I examined my own thoughts, desires, behaviors, motives, and attitudes in light of Scripture and God's mandate for holiness?
- Is my obedience to God motivated primarily by genuine spiritual passion, or by fear?
- In what ways do I cling to self-protection, false intimacy, and security?
- Do I find more joy in comfortable circumstances and loving relationships than I do in a deep communion with God?
- How often do I pretend that life is better than it really is?
- How do I handle such problems as resentment, lack of love, sexual urges, and fear?
- How do I respond to disappointment in relationships?
- In what ways can I clearly identify deceitfulness in my heart?
- Can I identify any sinful ways that I choose to relieve the pain in my life?
- How does the emptiness in my own being affect how I relate to others and to God?

■ Is my enjoyment of God greater than the blessing I receive from relationships with other people?

In addition to wrestling with these questions, I strongly recommend that anyone who undertakes a ministry of healing to sex addicts complete the recommended readings in appendix A (page 195).

Awareness of Our Own Sinfulness

As in all intense battles, there will be casualties and risks in ministering to those caught in sexual addiction, but the reward of moving into a sex addict's inner chambers is to know the thrill of going where no one has gone before. Many people have kept their sexual behaviors secret for years and have struggled unsuccessfully to gain victory over them, but few have ever addressed the deep crevasses of the whoring heart. Entering the battle from the perspective of addressing the sin of the heart requires increasing dependence on God along the path of spiritual growth. In many ways, dealing with a sex addict is not unfamiliar territory, for the issues plaguing the heart of the addict plague all of us as well.

You can't be prepared for the ministry of healing until you have dealt with your own struggles, including sexual ones, and explored the sinfulness of your heart. It is critical for you to be able to admit, with conviction, that your internal sexual issues and the dynamics of your heart are similar to those of the sex addict. When you begin to question how anyone could commit such sinful behaviors, or become irritated, surprised, or embarrassed by what someone has described doing sexually, it's time to reflect further on your own heart. When you truly understand sin, you'll realize there is nothing new or ultimately shocking about sexual addiction. Although you and I may be shocked by some behaviors, spiritual adultery is the more obscene picture.

Commitment to Confidentiality

By law, people who undertake a ministry of healing to sex addicts must treat what they learn about counselees with confidentiality. Confidentiality, which protects not only the sex addict but also his or her family and the church, is more a reflection of spiritual maturity than legislated restraint. Those who gossip about or slander others reveal their own sinfulness. They indicate that they are not suited to participate in such a delicate yet demanding ministry as helping sex addicts receive restoration.

I could share a number of illustrations that demonstrate why confidentiality is important and what happens when trust is violated, but I don't think it's necessary to do so here. When we put ourselves in a sex addict's position, or in the position of anyone who is struggling with sinful behavior, I think we each know deep down why confidentiality is vital to the healing process.

Commitment to God-Empowered Love

As believers, we are to express hatred of evil by withdrawing from it and abhorring it, not taking revenge on the sinner. To be used by God in the ministry of healing is to do battle with the real enemy, evil, and to love others. As God's children, you and I are called to spiritual intimacy and involvement with others for their good.

Within each of us lies the tendency to want people to pay for their sins—especially if they commit sins against us or someone we love. But God calls us to overcome evil with good. He calls us to be involved in restoration, not in vengeful acts: "Do not take revenge, my friends, but leave room for God's wrath, for it is written: 'It is mine to avenge; I will repay,' says the Lord. . . . Do not be overcome by evil, but overcome evil with good" (Romans 12:19-21). Each of us involved in the ministry of healing must be willing to love sex addicts through the power of God, surprising them with what they don't deserve and offering them the mercy, forgiveness, and joy only God can provide.

Loving those who are sexually addicted in the power of God's love entails a process of offering them what is *not* deserved so they might be restored to our Lord, to others, and to us. Properly understood, love is the greatest gift each of us can offer. When love is given to those held captive by the sins of sexual addiction and spiritual adultery, it reaches out with God's power to astound sinners. It destroys the power of sin over their lives. It contradicts all the false intimacy within sexual addiction and calls forth sinners to express true love because they have been loved so deeply.

Such a love is not weak. It requires courage, power, strength, and humility of heart. It is willing to engage in ministry regardless of the cost or the calculated chance of victory. It calls us to forsake emotional safety, motivates us to selflessness, and empowers us to respond in humble dependence on God. Such a love is a natural response to gaining from God what we don't deserve, which frees us to give the same to others. This love can then confront the sins of sexual addiction and spiritual adultery, regardless of the sex addict's response.

Focus on Sin, Not on Sexual Behavior

Sexually addictive behavior is often life-threatening and can seem incredibly foolish to someone who hasn't recognized the depths of sin. Sex addicts are at times arrogant and boastful, uttering words that could be likened to the breath of a wild predator savoring his recent prey.

You must not be repelled by what is at first visible in sex addicts' lives; the place of ministry lies much deeper within their hearts. Getting through the door of visible behavior will seem as if half the battle has been won, but it hasn't. Later battles will bring this first skirmish into perspective. *If Satan can engage you here at the door, the real battle may be lost.*

If you concentrate all your efforts on dealing with the sex addict's destructive and out-of-control behavior without engaging in direct battle with the adulterous heart that tries to manage relational pain, you may succeed on the external level but lose the battle. The "recovering" sex addict's pain and disappointment will continue to motivate him or her to seek distance in relationships, assume "normal" levels of false intimacy, and engage in other forms of self-protective behavior.

As an example, let's say a sex addict has participated in false intimacy with prostitutes or women on the other end of a 900 number. After his actions are discovered and a church leader has confronted him, the addict renounces his behavior. On the surface, the sexual behavior appears to be under control and the church leader believes that the addict has been healed. Yet the addict continues to use self-protective approaches. He avoids emotional risk by not initiating sexual relations with his wife. He avoids being alone with his closest friends and having to share intimate things about himself. He doesn't know how to listen to others and understand their feelings and thoughts. If conversation with his children strays to an uncomfortable subject, he changes it or leaves the room. Although his addictive behavior has been altered, nothing has changed on a deeper level.

Focus on Repentance

The ministry of healing requires an emphasis on repentance at the deepest levels of the heart. Because false intimacy is predictable and efficient in controlling relational pain, it becomes so powerful that the insanity of the sex addict's behavior can go far beyond his or her awareness. Trapped in the use of such power and control, a sex addict naturally does not experience the "godly sorrow" that is necessary for repentance and true internal and external change (see 2 Corinthians 7:9-11).

The godly sorrow that leads to repentance can begin to take hold of the soul only when the sex addict faces the ravages of sin and recognizes through the grace of God that the addictive behaviors are sinful. Godly sorrow develops when the sex addict gains a small hint of true intimacy and knows deep inside that the false intimacy is hollow, shallow, and bizarre.

A married man, for example, who feels godly sorrow while in a prostitute's arms remembers with passion and concern the time his wife held him. He begins to identify that he is empty, and the prostitute's touch becomes revolting. He remembers that at one time his wife offered much more. He realizes that the prostitute is a counterfeit and that he has been a fool.

Addicts who experience godly sorrow recognize that their foolishness is spiritual adultery that strips them away from the rich and fulfilling relationship God offers. Simultaneously, they are astonished by God's merciful offer of loving relationship — the opposite of what they deserve. Filled with repentance, their souls are stirred by legitimate shame as they confront their foolishness. *How could I have been enticed,* they ask themselves in so many words, *by a prostitute, a seductive voice on the phone, or a glossy piece of paper?*

THE FRAMEWORK OF HEALING
Recognize that Relief Will Not Be Immediate

Our culture, including many aspects of Christian subculture, offers relational relief *now*. This reassuring message comes through many promises of improved self-image, prosperity, even answered prayer. Tapes, books, seminars, and even sermons emphasizing the possibility of diminishing relational pain and healing personal wounds *now* are dispensed like so many over-the-counter pills.

In many ways, the church falsifies spiritual reality by pretending that people's lives can be nearly perfect in this fallen world. Examining this issue, Larry Crabb challenges the false attitude that "something we can do will advance us to a level of spirituality that eliminates pain and struggle as ongoing, deeply felt realities."[1] Such an attitude, common to the spiritual adulterer, states that we can do something to stop relational pain and find satisfaction once and for all.

At first glance my next statement may seem strange and cynical, but it's not intended to be: *I believe that Christianity has sometimes been packaged and marketed to meet the same autonomous desires within the lustful heart that the prostitute's erotic offer of sex promises to meet in the heart of a lonely man.* Let me explain this further. The real message of the whore is not unlike that of Satan's message to Eve: "You can have it, and you can have it pain-free." The same false belief exists, the same deceptive promise is made, and the same base seduction takes place.

Within Christianity, some people offer similar "we can do it" solutions to the problems of living. "Relief through Christ is there for the taking. Come on and take it. It's yours. You can ease the pain of life by renewing your efforts in Christian living. God will bless you; He guarantees to do so, and He will do it now." It's ironic that a distorted message of the gospel appealing to our naturally autonomous hearts can fertilize the seeds of sin. The appeal is subtle, for often what we desire from God seems so legitimate. Therefore, we reason, God must provide it.

We can't prevent the problems of sexual addiction within the church if we don't change our message from "how to feel better now" to the unpopular biblical theme that the sufferings we now experience "are not worth comparing with the glory that will be revealed in us" (Romans 8:18). We must emphasize the message of patience, endurance, perseverance, and hope rather than the message of immediate healing for the wounds of life. We must teach spiritual groaning rather than tacitly encouraging spiritual murmuring when God doesn't seem to be meeting our needs today.

Groaning is waiting. It is an expression of the travail of the heart for that moment of union. It comes with a deep sigh that is sustained by a living hope. This embryonic hope, which dwells deeply within the heart, is a guarantee of the eternal life that is to come in Christ. When such a hope is vibrantly alive in a person, spiritual adultery is unthinkable. Preventing sexual addiction within the church isn't possible until we believe that God is good and worth waiting for.

Practice Loving Confrontation

It's disturbing to hear members of a congregation admit to having been suspicious or aware of their pastor's sexual misconduct after his behaviors become public, but it's all too typical. Often we have suspicions but prefer not to think the worst. Sadly, this attitude usually stems from the fact that we don't take sin in other people seriously because we don't take sin in ourselves seriously. Often we find ourselves involved in relationships in which we are more concerned with comfort and enjoyment than with offering a love that confronts sinful behavior and attitudes.

I know how easy it is to follow the more comfortable choice. While having dinner with close friends, Rosemary and I quickly recognized that the wife was using coercion and manipulation to influence her family's decisions. She was clearly insensitive and self-centered. But did I say anything to her about it? No. To my shame, I failed to become involved. I feared the loss of an enjoyable evening and the difficulty of having to deal with a negative response to what I should have said. Looking back on that time, I have asked myself, *Were you more concerned with your comfort or with the lives of your friends?*

As you minister to sex addicts, you will obviously have to confront them concerning their sin. But confrontation must always be an act of love, stemming from your awareness that in God's eyes your own sin is just as abhorrent as the sin of a sex addict. You should not confront others with the attitude of "How could you?" — which indirectly expresses the anger implied in it. The purpose of confrontation is not merely to deal with the hurt that the sex addict has caused others. It's not simply to "get rid" of sinful behaviors. Although genuine confrontation never denies the seriousness of the sex addict's offenses, it is done for one reason only: *to restore the sex addict's relationship with God, self, and others.* Only a confrontation in love will compel a sex addict to face his or her internal disease of sin: spiritual adultery.

Confrontation in love surprises the sex addict and leads to the possibility of his or her repentance. However, be assured that confrontation for the purpose of healing will be met with resistance. Anticipate resistance and self-justification when you move courageously against the forces of evil. Remember that in many instances sex addicts have known the truth about God. They have been aware of the destructiveness of their behavior yet have been unable to bring it under control. They have been driven by the powerful underlying motivation to manage and control relational pain.

Empowered by God's Spirit and motivated by the desire for the sex addict's restoration, you must creatively weave through the multitude of consequences that the sex addict's behavior has caused. When you face resistance as a result of loving confrontation, avoid the tendency to react scornfully, to feel as if it's time to punish not only the sexual behavior but the sex addict's stubbornness. It's simple to say but difficult to practice: You must deal with the resistance by asking God to search your heart further, and then respond with great strength and determination to help the sex addict receive restoration.

Model and Seek a Response of Brokenness
A key goal of the ministry of healing is *to help the sex addict experience brokenness.* Genuine change for a sex addict begins with brokenness, which includes a deep sense of helplessness, a penetrating godly sorrow, and a desperate grasping for God.

A stark change in direction, brokenness is a form of humility. The sex addict deeply acknowledges his or her inability to control relational pain and find fulfillment without God. Seized by the horror of the insanity that has spawned such arrogance toward God, facing the insanity and the inability to find self-fulfillment, the sex addict is pushed to make a choice: to strive for further control or to faint at God's feet and relinquish self-protective ways of response. Legitimate shame resulting from an awareness of his or her foolishness can awaken the sex addict to the piercing sense of helplessness. At that moment, he or she can fall trembling before God, deserving nothing less than death for sins committed and yet at that moment being startled by God's astounding grace.

The prophet addressed stubbornness, the opposite of brokenness: "You were wearied by all your ways, but you would not say, 'It is hopeless.' You found renewal of your strength, and so you did not faint" (Isaiah 57:10). When we are broken, we each say to God, in effect, "It's hopeless and nothing I can do on my own will work," and then we faint at His feet. In the ministry of healing, we each can exhibit brokenness by humbly delighting in loving and serving the sex addict even when the return or reward is at best uncertain.

SUMMARY

The problem of sexual addiction within the church is only the tip of the iceberg. There are more sex addicts with secret sins than we care to imagine, but the issue is more critical than even this reality. I pray and hope that this book will help the church become more aware of sexual addiction and motivate people to become involved in the ministry of healing to sex addicts. However, even this ambitious objective is insignificant in light of the great need for Christians to realize that *sexual addiction and many other problems are the direct result of spiritual adultery.*

In some ways the church can be likened to a couple I counseled. Their marriage looked good on the outside. Other couples admired their relationship. They never fought, and they did everything a Christian couple was supposed to do. The wife was kind, respectful, and stood loyally by her husband's side. But she hadn't made love to her husband for many years. She lacked passion, due to deep resentment that had festered within her. She had received many benefits from being a good wife, but internally she mistrusted her husband's goodness. She had never been in another man's arms, but in her heart she was unfaithful.

Obviously God didn't intend marriages to be passionless. Likewise, the church can do many things correctly, such as developing correct programs, teaching sound doctrine, and training effective Sunday school teachers. From the outside, the church can appear to be great. But what's on the inside matters the most. As believers, we must choose to be faithful to God and refuse to bow to the subtle and blatant forces that urge us to seek our own fulfillment, to become spiritually adulterous. We must minister in love to others in need and remain faithful and pure in our relationship to God as we guide others away from sin toward His healing grace and mercy.

I believe that the serious crisis of sexual addiction within the clergy confirms the extent to which spiritual adultery exists within the church. In the next chapter, let's take a practical look at how the church should deal with Christian leaders who have fallen morally and with the consequences of their sexual behaviors.

✦ 9 ✦

Healing for Christian Leaders

A s the morning worship service began, the senior pastor was conspicuously absent. Already church members were asking questions, since he had been unavailable for days. Then the chairman of the board of elders stepped up to the pulpit, opened in prayer, and in a tired voice began to read the following letter, which I've reproduced:

> Dear Congregation,
> With painful regret and a deep measure of grief, the leadership of First Church [name changed] must inform you that our senior pastor, Dr. Lawrence Thomas [name changed], has been relieved of his pastoral duties. Dr. Thomas is struggling with moral failure and needs an extended period of time to seek help and healing.

The moment stunned the members of the congregation with instantaneous feelings of shock, disbelief, fear, betrayal, and compassion. "I just don't believe it. Our pastor wouldn't do that!" some said. "How could anyone do this and risk destroying the ministry of our church?" others asked. "I feel for his poor wife and children. How will they ever make it through this?" still others wondered.

The situation was particularly painful for staff members and elders, who were losing sleep from the tragedy itself and the burden of decisionmaking that was forced upon them. Questions agonized the thoughts of everyone involved: "How could this have happened?" "How do we handle all the questions?" "Did we do the right thing?"

❖   ❖   ❖

Dealing with a fallen public figure in ministry is a task for which few of us are prepared ahead of time. It's a bit like planning a funeral for a particular date and making all the arrangements before the person scheduled for burial is even dead. However, I believe that churches and Christian organizations need to prepare in advance for a leader's moral failure so they can handle the situation effectively and in a godly manner.

A survey of pastors by the Fuller Institute of Church Growth indicated that "thirty-seven percent have been involved in inappropriate sexual behavior with someone in the church."[1] Evidence indicates that this shocking and disturbing statistic is true. I frequently receive calls for counseling from Christian leaders around the country who have "fallen" — who are sexually addicted or have been involved in sexual misconduct.

Earlier in this book, I offered some opinions on the causes of sexual addiction. These same causes apply to clergy. Clergy and lay leaders are not immune to the same internal drive of sin, the same arrogance, the same self-protective behaviors, the same demand to avoid pain, and the same desire for false intimacy that affect other people. In fact, Christian leaders may be more prone to suffering from the problems of sexual addiction due to the unique strategies they often employ to manage relationships and life's pressures. Consider the following characteristics that often apply to clergy:

- A higher probability of isolation and loneliness.
- A tendency to neglect normal interpersonal relations for the sake of ministry, which results in poor marital relations.
- A common lack of ongoing feedback from others that results in a lack of serious heart searching.

- The tendency accompanying professionalism and power to repress relational pain that results in increased vulnerability to illicit sexual relations.
- Tendency to equate the passion for the work of ministry to spiritual passion for God.
- A belief that separation required in the ministry includes emotional distance from others.
- Efforts to heal the wounds of life ineffectively through ministry service.
- Experiencing numbing relational pain, but possibly attempting to recapture a sense of emotional vitality by feeling another's pain through counseling.
- Suffering a loss of genuine intimacy but possibly attempting to recover it by always being available to others.
- Tendency to maintain a sense of control over life's difficult issues by insisting on the right theology.

Christian leaders are sometimes great externalists. On the outside they can be models of what devoted Christians are supposed to be, yet inside remain self-indulgent. Quite often, for example, a young seminary student or pastor neglects his internal spiritual condition when preparing for ministry. Upon graduation from seminary and receiving ordination, the young pastor is placed on a pedestal of respect, considered to be a spiritual authority, and becomes the recipient of trust — all of which result in relational distance, unrealistic expectations, and a setup for future problems.

The pastor and the congregation can use this arrangement to create a type of false intimacy. For the pastor, it provides an immediate sense of acceptance and respect. For the congregation, it provides someone they can believe in to be available to meet their needs. This context creates a breeding ground for a fallen personality structure in which a person demands to ease the pain and wounds of life without God. Such an arrangement feeds a sex addict's demand and sense of entitlement to have personal needs met. Place these factors into the context of isolation, and it's not surprising that sexual addiction is common among clergy and Christian leaders in general.

Important and unique questions arise when church leaders and others must minister to a Christian leader who has fallen morally. In the remainder of this chapter, I will provide practical answers to many of these questions. Because many questions address sexual addiction that has involved some type of physical contact, I will generally define physical contact to include touching genital areas or breasts, with or without clothing on, for the purpose of sexual stimulation or gratification. The partner may or may not be a willing participant. Sexual misconduct may also involve the use of a leadership position to sexually abuse a person verbally or to engage in any type of intrusive sexual behavior.

Can a Christian leader who has sexually sinned be restored to the office of ministry? Scripture does not clearly prohibit the restoration of a fallen Christian leader. Therefore, opinions and strong disagreements about restoration abound within the church.

A key point to keep in mind here is that *spiritual adultery is the core issue.* Blatant sexual sin is a reflection of spiritual adultery, but spiritual adultery isn't always reflected by blatant sexual sin. Although "all our righteous acts are like filthy rags" (Isaiah 64:6), when a Christian leader is involved in sexual sin there is a unique violation of trust. Sexual sins often violate or damage others, and nowhere is this more true than when a Christian leader commits sexual sin. In addition to damaging others—a spouse, a victim, and family members—the leader sins against God and damages the name and the Body of Christ.

A number of passages in Scripture provide specific qualifications for Christian leaders. These passages indicate the type of character that is required before a Christian enters a leadership position and the high standards that he or she must maintain after leadership responsibilities are assumed.

In 1 Timothy 3:2, Paul wrote that a Christian leader must be "above reproach." This person must do nothing that will provide grounds for accusation. This person must be "blameless" (Titus 1:6) and lead an exemplary life that can withstand full scrutiny. As the "husband of but one wife" (1 Timothy 3:2, Titus 1:6), or the wife of one husband, this leader should have a godly character, should know the richness of genuine marital intimacy, and should isolate the expression of intimate love to his or her spouse. Such a leader is morally pure.

When a Christian leader fails to meet biblical standards, he or she is disqualified to serve. Spiritual restoration is required (Galatians 6:1-2), and he or she is to be removed from the office of ministry.

Scripture does not reveal whether or not a fallen leader can requalify for leadership. Since no prohibition is given, we can assume that requalification can take place, but only following a time of restoration during which the person must prove his or her character.

How should a leader who is suspected of moral failure be confronted? At this point, it's important to make a clear distinction between false accusations and clearly evident sin. When spiritual leaders meet the qualifications of being above reproach and blameless, the church is to prevent such leaders from facing false accusations. (See 1 Timothy 5:19-20, Matthew 18:15-17, 2 Corinthians 13:1.) Clearly, false accusations lead to dissension, discouragement, and other harmful consequences.

When grounds exist for the accusations, disciplinary action should be taken. An elder, for instance, must be dealt with strongly for the sake of warning other elders (1 Timothy 5:20). This public approach to sin conflicts with the opinions of others, but I believe that it creates a healthy fear of sin and sin's disgraceful consequences.

In order for the accusations to be verified and disciplinary action to be taken, the fallen leader must be confronted. Church policy may require that the leader's immediate supervisor be involved. In a multi-staffed, independent church, perhaps the chairman of the elder board or the senior staff person will be involved. Most likely the confrontation will also involve the person who has direct information regarding the sinful behavior.

During the confrontation, it's best to solicit information rather than reveal it. In other words, ask a question such as, "We've received reliable information that you've been involved in sexual misconduct. How would you respond to this? Would you like to confess the full extent of the problem?" Often only one aspect of the leader's sexual sins will have surfaced first. If you approach the issue with this type of open-ended questions, the leader may admit not only what you know, but much more.

What if the leader admits past sexual sins as well as current ones? When past sexual problems are revealed, it's imperative that you investigate them. Determine if a restoration process was initiated and completed. Determine if the types of sinful behaviors the leader was previously involved in have resurfaced or changed. Perhaps the problems were undetected or the restoration process was ignored or mismanaged previously.

Should all types of sexual sin be announced and dealt with publicly in the church? The issue of public disclosure depends on the type of sexual sin committed and whether or not other people have been impacted — spiritually, mentally, emotionally, or physically. If at least one other person within the church or the leader's family has been negatively impacted in a serious way, the matter should be made public. Covering up the sin breeds rumors and works as a cancer in the ongoing ministry of the church, not to mention that it allows the fallen leader to continue on in sin and perhaps hurt other people.

If the sin is made public, details of the leader's sexual behavior should be omitted but the seriousness of the problem should be emphasized. Terms such as "serious moral failure," "sexual sin," or even "sexual addiction" can be used when appropriate. Typically, the congregation will want to verify that the information is true, and making it public provides such validation. Another church leader may read a written, general statement, with or without the fallen leader being present. Or the fallen leader or an appropriate church leader such as the chairman of the elder board may read a letter of confession. Smaller, more private meetings may also be held, during which members of the congregation can ask questions and receive answers.

If the sexual sin is not intrusive, it may or may not be publicly revealed before the congregation. For instance, the sin of a pastor who is addicted to masturbation and pornography and has not victimized anyone else may be publicly revealed before a small group of elders or godly people who will assist him privately to overcome the addiction. Although nonintrusive forms of sexual addition should not be minimized, public discipline may not be required.

When masturbation affects the leader's ability to fulfill the requirements of ministry, a thirty-day leave may greatly assist the healing process. In severe cases, the leader may require out-patient or in-patient treatment by a professional counselor.

But the sin of a pastor who has had sexual relations with a counselee or member of the congregation must be publicly revealed before the whole church. Obviously no one formula applies here. It's important for the church leaders to prayerfully seek God's guidance before determining which type of public disclosure is required. Note that the sin should be publicly revealed, not publicly punished, and that public exposure doesn't necessarily mean expulsion from the life of the congregation will always follow. Expulsion could result if the person is unrepentant.

Often, not knowing what else to do, a church in this situation prefers to turn the matter over to an "expert." This person, who may provide helpful assistance and wisdom, should be viewed as a useful resource but should not replace or be a substitute for the actions of other church leaders or the restoration process directed by the restoration committee.

Does this mean that a restoration committee should be formed? If so, who should be on it? Yes, a restoration committee is a proven, effective way to deal with a Christian leader's moral failure. A church's willingness to help restore its fallen members, leaders or not, is a mark of its spiritual health.

Whether or not a fallen leader ever returns to an official ministry position, a restoration process should take place to deal with his sin and heal his soul. Only spiritually mature people who are deeply committed to the leader and to implementing the philosophy and goals of the church or denomination should serve on the restoration committee. If the leader is well known, the church should consider appointing someone outside the church to the committee, such as a local pastor who has good rapport with the fallen leader. Each person who considers serving should count the personal cost—the time that will be taken away from other duties, family, and leisure.

A committee comprising three to five people will be ideal. In a committee of this small size, the members will be more likely to become relationally close and to communicate with one another easily outside of scheduled meetings.

Who controls the restoration process? To a large extent the control of the restoring process is determined by church policy. Written policies should determine authority; otherwise, difficulties may arise when a restoration committee reports to someone else or a committee of elders. The restoration committee should determine when spiritual restoration is complete. Should reinstatement to the office of ministry be an option, another committee or board that normally has the authority to ordain or credential people will become involved.

How often should the committee meet with the fallen leader? In the early stages of restoration, weekly meetings may be required. Eventually the meetings may be held monthly, with all members present. In between scheduled monthly meetings, each committee member should have face-to-face and telephone contact with the leader.

However, I recommend that any committee members who are of the opposite sex from the leader keep personal contact to a minimum to avoid the appearance of evil. At least once a week, a member of the committee should personally visit the leader, and all committee members should be available to him or her if support, counsel, or special prayer is requested.

How long should the process of restoration take? There is no optimum time frame for the restoration process. The best answer may be, "As long as is necessary." On one level time is not an issue, since the healing process can't be compressed into a certain time period and the seriousness of the leader's sin is not the only issue that will need to be dealt with during restoration. However, I recommend that restoration be carried out for a minimum of one year. It takes time for each of us to build character, and sexual addiction reflects a deep character problem. Sometimes a longer period of healing is needed, as much as five years.

It's important that the church not cut short the restoration process because of financial pressure or pressure from other people, including the pastor and/or his family. Often a fallen pastor wants to return to the ministry quickly because he feels lost without a pulpit, needs a job, and wants the whole restoration process to end. Quite often, though, his desire or demand to move quickly is a warning sign that the restoration process is incomplete. It takes time.

Is the church responsible to assist financially in the cost of restoration? Should it continue providing a salary? A number of factors—including emotions, theology, and personal walk with God—influence the extent to which the church or Christian organization will respond financially. Also, health insurance policies vary widely. Some pay for in-patient and/or out-patient counseling. Others pay no counseling costs or cover only a limited number of sessions.

Personally, I believe that financial assistance is a critical part of the ministry of healing. A church should take its commitment to minister to the sinner and those who are wounded seriously. Often, sacrificial financial help is necessary in order for the leader (and other family members) to receive effective counseling and pay additional travel and housing costs that may be incurred if effective counseling can't take place locally.

At the least, I suggest that if an insurance policy covers the cost of counseling, the church should continue to pay the policy's premiums for the length of the restoration process.

To aid in the restoration process and avoid placing additional pressure on the fallen leader, I recommend that the church or Christian organization extend his or her full salary for six months or until new employment is obtained, whichever comes first.

What if the leader continues to commit sexual sin or is unrepentant? How long should the church or organization be willing to offer help for restoration? When the Christian leader is unrepentant, permanent expulsion from the position of ministry is required (1 Corinthians 5). This would likely include termination of salary and benefits within a short period of time. However, it's important to pray for the leader and his or her reconciliation with God and others, and to be willing to begin the restoration process should the leader repent before the final decision of termination is made.

If the leader has been sexually involved with a staff person, how does that affect the restoration process? Restoration for both parties is required. Any time a secretary or other non-ordained staff person has been sexually involved with a Christian leader, I believe it's appropriate to request the leader's resignation and the resignation of the staff member. This makes a statement regarding the seriousness of sin and the mark it places on the church's reputation.

Could the church or denomination be legally liable as a result of the leader's sin? Much depends on the exact nature of the moral failure in determining legal issues. Obviously solitary masturbation has no legal liability, but sexual molestation of a counselee or other intrusive behavior does.

Whenever the fallen leader's actions have affected another person, a lawsuit is a possibility regardless of whether the evidence is strong or weak. All that's needed is someone who believes he or she has a case and a lawyer who is willing to handle the case and file the paperwork in the court system.

The best approach to potential lawsuits is to be prepared to defend the church or Christian organization in court. You can't prevent a lawsuit, but you can protect yourself from losing a case. Your best defense is to have a well-managed, comprehensive restoration process that is ready to be used. When a restoration process is in place and well documented, you'll be able to demonstrate the church's intent to deal with the problem correctly and show that the church handled this particular matter appropriately should such behavior occur again.

First, *develop written policies and procedures on sexual misconduct ahead of time* that demonstrate your intent to prevent such problems and to deal with them if they occur. Become aware of the laws in your state regarding issues such as reporting suspected child abuse and the sexual misconduct of a professional. More and more states are passing laws regarding sexual misconduct by someone in a professional position of trust, and such behavior may be criminal.

Next, *document the work of the restoration committee.* This is important to establish proper management of the situation. Documentation includes: dates, times, places, issues discussed, decisions made and the reasons why they were made. Include any reports prepared by a professional therapist or treatment program that is involved in restoration. This documentation will support the fact that the lengthy restoration process was managed appropriately and will allow committee members to review all steps.

This question only summarizes some of the legal issues a church may face in the event of allegations of clergy misconduct. If your church is confronted with such an allegation, it is highly recommended that you consult with an attorney who is experienced in this area of the law.

Which sexual behaviors should be reported to state or local agencies? You need to know your state laws and who is required to report child abuse, sexual misconduct, or sexual exploitation. For example, in Colorado I would be required to report to the state if an adult woman under my care tells me that she has been sexually involved with a licensed or unlicensed counselor and releases me to report it. Regardless of the state laws, it may be appropriate to report the sexual behavior to the proper agencies or authorities, particularly when the behavior has been intrusive.

Do not cover up or ignore any allegations of sexual abuse, sexual misconduct, or sexual exploitation. Deal with such allegations immediately, or they may surface years later after an incident occurs. A sixteen-year-old girl who was sexually involved with her youth pastor never told anyone about the abuse until five years later when she entered therapy and shared the full story with her therapist, who encouraged her to report the incident to the pastor's denomination. These types of occurrences will become more common as more people courageously deal with abuse they have suffered at the hands of others.

What is the best way to handle the negative publicity that will occur? Since I began working with victims of sexual abuse and with sex addicts, I've been involved in about a dozen cases in which the news media took interest. Rarely does the media ever tell the story accurately. Avoid publicity if you can, but recognize that in many cases it's unavoidable. If someone is arrested, for instance, all court proceedings are a matter of public record and newspapers can easily find and run the story.

If you are fairly certain that the story will become public, you may choose to prepare a written statement, make it available on request, and decline to answer further questions. Or you may appoint someone who can capably answer all media-related questions, deal with hostile interviewers, and handle the intense pressure. Defer all questions and face-to-face interviews to that person only.

If the leader's spouse and/or children don't know about the sexual misconduct, should they be told? Who should do so, and how much should be revealed? One of the hardest parts of my job in working with fallen pastors and Christian leaders is to be involved in sharing the nature of the sexual offense(s) with unsuspecting spouses and older children. Yet the dishonesty must not be allowed to continue.

The fallen leader should reveal the full extent of his or her behavioral problem(s). If, for instance, the leader has had multiple affairs, he or she must provide the specific number, not just state that an affair has taken place. Most spouses will ask for this information anyway, and there is no excuse for lying about the facts. But there is also a point at which too much truth can be hurtful.

As a rule of thumb, I recommend that the fallen leader answer direct questions with direct answers. When possible, general categories of behaviors should be revealed, such as participation in prostitution, pornography, topless bars, 900 calls, sexual abuse, etc. Graphic details should not be provided, however, for they only cause undue pain.

The restoration committee should encourage the leader to tell his or her children without dictating what is to be revealed. I personally believe that if a fallen leader's children are teenagers or older, he or she, and the spouse, should disclose the sexual misconduct to them. The pain the children experience when being informed of the situation by their parents is not nearly as difficult to bear as the pain that is suffered when the truth is delivered through malicious statements or rumors.

In what ways should the church become involved in the restoration of the leader's spouse and/or family? Taking the ministry of restoration seriously means that the entire immediate family will be included in the restoration process. Individual counseling for the fallen leader is required. If he or she is married, counseling is also required for the spouse and older children.

Each member of the family, excluding very young children, will need caring support during this difficult time, not isolation and the withdrawal of friends and colleagues. I recommend that a small group of selected people maintain daily contact with family members, both by phone and in person. Give the family privacy, but don't allow the fear of being an imposition to limit meaningful contact.

What if the spouse wants a divorce? None of us can stop a spouse from obtaining a divorce. However, the restoration committee should encourage the spouse of the fallen leader to work toward forgiveness and reconciliation, since the restoration process will address the marital problems and assist in reconciling the husband and wife.

When should a pastor be asked to resign? Each situation will need to be judged individually. The primary issue at hand is the level of spiritual adultery—the hardness of the heart, the lack of passion for God. Other issues include laws that may have been broken and the injury or potential injury to at least one other person.

In my view, whenever there has been any physical sexual contact, even if it was fondling without sexual intercourse, resignation is required. Physical sexual contact is not only a violation of Scripture but indicates serious breaches of trust and serious character flaws that may include even greater exploitation of others.

Some types of sexual addiction that have not involved physical contact may not require resignation. However, some sex addicts, while they have never had physical contact with someone, act out sexual behavior at levels that indicate not just a loss of control but an obsession that would naturally bring the spiritual condition of their hearts into question. Therefore, some sex addicts who have engaged in verbal sexual contact by phone or in person should be asked to resign.

Remember, resignation is not a punishment. It's a recognition of the seriousness of the spiritual problem that disqualifies the fallen leader and/or reduces his or her ministry effectiveness. A leader who resigns should still be involved in a process of personal restoration over an extended period of time.

Is a leave of absence a viable alternative to resignation? A leave of absence can enhance spiritual restoration and is appropriate with some levels of sexually addictive behavior. But the church should not grant a leave of absence simply to avoid dealing with the effects of a resignation.

If the leader resigns, should he or she leave town? The smaller the town, the more essential it is for the leader to leave, to protect the church and his or her family. Should the leader decide to move, the church should do everything it can to ensure that the restoration process will continue following the move.

Does restoration include the leader's marital relationship? Yes! In every sexual addiction case in which the addict I've counseled was married, significant marital issues needed to be resolved. Marriage counseling should be a required part of the restoration process. In some cases, the marriage tragically ends in divorce. But regardless of the outcome, restoration should include an attempt to bring full healing to the marital relationship.

If the church or Christian organization determines that the leader can resume his or her responsibilities after the restoration process has been concluded, should the restoration be ended publicly? Yes, I highly recommend that a public restoration service be held at the conclusion of the restoration process. The service will be a time of closure, healing, and celebration of God's mercy. The service should be held even if the leader does not wish to return to the office of ministry.

Should the leader who completes restoration return to the same congregation or organization? Often people's inability to deal with sexual behavior problems will require that both the leader and the congregation or organization have a fresh start after the restoration process is completed. Ideally, I can imagine the leader being restored, the congregation or organization experiencing healing, and the whole process resulting in such a powerful spiritual revival that returning to the same office of ministry would be appropriate. However, in the real world, levels of bitterness, resentment, and lack of understanding usually require the leader to change churches or move to another organization.

Should a sex addict return to the same type of ministry? When his or her sexual addiction has involved a violation of trust within a counseling relationship, the fallen leader must not return to a counseling ministry. Likewise, if sexually addictive behaviors occurred primarily in the context of a traveling ministry, the leader should not return to such ministry. Often a pastor who is a sex addict is a workaholic, too. In this case, the pastor must drastically change his work schedules. When the leader has neglected his or her marriage, the marital relationship should be carefully monitored even after the leader has completed the restoration process.

In short, sexual addiction never occurs alone as a manifestation of spiritual adultery. Therefore, expect that the fallen leader, and perhaps others, will need to make changes in such areas as money management, parenting, relationship with spouse, relationships with staff members, time management, time spent in isolation, and lack of accountability.

How can we tell if the leader really has changed? As I point out in other chapters of this book, external assessment alone is not only inadequate but fails to address deeper spiritual issues. God alone is capable of searching the motives, the intent, and the passions of the heart. Real change on the inside is reflected by external change, but external change doesn't necessarily indicate genuine internal change. The leader must shift his or her perception of the source of fulfillment that in turn changes his or her approach to relationships and life in general.

A primary indicator of positive change is the quality of relationship that a person in restoration is able to offer others, especially those closest to him or her. Look for a new sense of humility, a new willingness to serve from highly different motives. The fruit of the Spirit must be exhibited: "love, joy, peace, patience, kindness, goodness, faithfulness, gentleness and self-control" (Galatians 5:22-23). Self-sacrifice, the primary ingredient, benefits others.

The issue of self-control, which is also important, seems rather strange in our culture—just as people in the days of the Apostle Paul viewed chastity as unreasonable. Many Greeks and Jews of his day found sexual satisfaction outside of marriage, so Paul wrote, "Avoid sexual immorality . . . each of you should learn to control his own body in a way that is holy and honorable, not in passionate lust like the heathen, who do not know God" (1 Thessalonians 4:3-5). It's important to note that self-control, not self-discipline, is directed inward. The person who exhibits self-control possesses (or owns) his or her desires and impulses (1 Corinthians 7:9).

Restoration involves much more than repentance and forgiveness for poor behavior. Restoration is a return to holiness at the deepest levels of the heart. A restored person will always appear wiser, more refined, and emotionally stronger. His or her strength will be illustrated by boasting "the more gladly about . . . weaknesses" and the "delight in . . . insults, in hardships, in persecutions, in difficulties" (2 Corinthians 12:9-10).

What if evidence of sexual misconduct surfaces years after the alleged sin(s) took place? An accusation of past sexual misconduct can't be ignored. It will affect the spiritual well-being of the church and the leader. It will rarely go away without intervention.

We can hope that the accusation was initiated by someone who desires restoration with the abuser, and the church must enter into that effort. More often than not, past sexual problems will have gone unacknowledged and the sex addict will not have dealt with them, so more of these cases may surface. As in the case of a current sexual sin, a restoration process needs to be initiated if evidence indicates that the accusation is true.

What are some early warning signs of sexual addiction that would require staff members, elders, or others to be concerned and approach the pastor or leader with frank questions? Asking frank questions may or may not reveal a problem with sexual addiction, but the answers may reveal other needs in the Christian leader's life. Only responsible persons who care deeply about the leader should use the material in this chapter, or ponder the following questions.

- Is the leader isolated and lonely? Does he or she have few friends?
- Is there noticeable stress in his or her marriage?
- Is the leader noticeably depressed, discouraged, or lacking in motivation?
- Is there a growing sense that the leader is unavailable to

others and unable to account for his or her time?
- Is the leader remiss in avoiding appearances of evil with members of the opposite or same sex?
- Have there been rumors of inappropriate relationships or sexual behaviors concerning the leader's life? Has he or she, for instance, been seen in suspicious places, such as a porno bookstore or gay bar?
- Does the leader have an especially close relationship with someone involved in the church, such as a church secretary? Have questions been asked about the leader's marital relationship?
- Does the leader hide behind a role to cover relational pain in his or her own life?

SUMMARY

Each situation requiring restoration is unique. No matter what the circumstances, the process of restoration will be excruciating. Emotions will be tense. Lives may be shattered. Careers may be ruined. Marriages may be destroyed. Ministries may be weakened. During times like this, cowardice only increases the devastation to the people involved.

Through the power of God and His abiding love and mercy, the church can be an instrument of healing. Expecting sin to abound in this world, the church can respond with courage to meet the needs of hurting leaders and those affected by their behaviors.

One final word is appropriate. If you are a Christian leader and have committed sexual sin, don't delay getting help. Seek out people who can help you and guide you toward restoration. Whatever the extent of your problem, hope and grace can abound.

When Christian leaders contact me anonymously, fearful they will lose their careers or hurt people close to them, I ask them, "How long can you hold out without asking for help? Even though it's never easy, wouldn't it be better to come forward now than be accused or even arrested later?" Your sexual sin will have consequences, but often you can control the seriousness of those consequences by coming forward on your own. May God give you courage.

✦A✦
Recommended Reading

Allender, Dan B. ***Bold Love***. Colorado Springs: NavPress, 1992.
A profound book that will greatly help the sex addict with the healing process and assist spouses of sex addicts in loving and forgiving.

— — — *The Wounded Heart*. Colorado Springs: NavPress, 1992.
Addresses the problem of adults who are victims of childhood sexual abuse and is very helpful in understanding how all of us deal with the wounds of a fallen world. A companion workbook is also available. It can be used by individuals or in a group setting.

Carnes, Patrick. ***Don't Call It Love: Recovery from Sexual Addiction.***
New York: Bantam Books, 1991.
A secular book by the foremost authority on sexual addiction, from candid testimony of more than one thousand former sex addicts. The information is helpful to counselors and others ministering to sex addicts.

— — — *Out of the Shadows*. Minneapolis: CompCare Publications, 1983.
A secular book that is considered to be the primer on sexual addiction.

Crabb, Larry. ***Inside Out***. Colorado Springs: NavPress, 1988.
Details the internal change process that is required in spiritual restoration.

— — —*Men and Women: Enjoying the Difference*. Grand Rapids: Zondervan Corporation, 1991.

> Provides a clear statement on male/female differences from a biblical perspective and valuable understanding of the core problem of self-centeredness.

— — —*Understanding People*. Grand Rapids: Zondervan Corporation, 1987.

> An excellent description of our fallen personality structure in terms of our longings, thinking, choices, and feelings.

Hayford, Jack. *Restoring Fallen Leaders*. Ventura, CA: Regal Books, 1988.

> A short book dealing with restoration of fallen Christian leaders.

Huggins, Kevin. *Parenting Adolescents*. Colorado Springs: NavPress, 1989.

> Although directed to parents of adolescents, the framework for effective parenting outlined in this book is a resource for all parents. It further develops the type of parenting required in a fallen world.

LaHaye, Tim. *If Ministers Fall, Can They be Restored?* Grand Rapids: Zondervan Corporation, 1990.

> Valuable information on thinking through the process of restoration. The book gives an overview of various opinions on the subject as well as practical advice that would be helpful in writing a policy to minister to fallen Christian leaders.

Rutter, Peter. *Sex in the Forbidden Zone*. Los Angeles: Jeremy P. Tarcher, Inc., 1989.

> A secular book that presents a good understanding of the problem of sexual exploitation by those in positions of trust and power, such as therapists, doctors, clergy, and teachers.

White, John, and Ken Blue. *Healing the Wounded: The Costly Love of Church Discipline*. Downers Grove, IL: InterVarsity Press, 1985.

> Stimulates thinking on the important subject of church discipline and guides anyone interested in a ministry of healing for fallen leaders.

APPENDIX

✦ B ✦

Ministry Resources

Dr. Harry W. Schaumburg
P.O. Box 26015
Colorado Springs, CO 80936

If you are interested in the sexual addiction ministry of the author, please write for information on the following:

- Seminars
- Sexual Addiction Recovery Week — a week-long intensive individual counseling program
- Couples Sexual Addiction Recovery Week — a week-long couple's week of intensive counseling
- In-patient Treatment Program — two to three weeks of hospital treatment with comprehensive evaluation and individual and group therapy

Dr. Schaumburg regrets that he is unable to answer individual letters.

❖   ❖   ❖

Life Enrichment
14581 East Tuffs Avenue
Aurora, CO 80015
(303)693-3954

Life Enrichment, directed by Wes Roberts, ministers to Christian leaders and maintains a network of experienced counselors in various parts of the country.

❖   ❖   ❖

Institute of Biblical Counseling
16075 West Belleview Avenue
Morrison, CO 80465

Dr. Larry Crabb and Dr. Dan B. Allender offer counselor training seminars and recovery workshops for survivors of sexual abuse. Write for a schedule of workshops and seminars.

Indicators of Sexual Abuse

PHYSICAL
- Unexplained torn, soiled, or bloody underwear
- Disruption of normal eating patterns
- Health problems, such as vomiting, headaches, allergies, rashes, unusual vaginal discharge, and unusual urinary tract infection
- Physical complaints such as stomachache, pain in the genital area, genital or anal irritation
- Sexually transmitted disease
- Soreness or injury to the genital area, anus, or mouth

BEHAVIORAL AND EMOTIONAL
- Unexplained irritability
- Unable to get along with others
- Sleep disorder, with or without bad dreams or nightmares
- Depressed, despondent, withdrawn, inactive, daydreaming, lack of concentration, unusually quiet
- Destructive behavior toward things or people
- Fearful of certain people or places
- Pleas of not being left alone or with someone or someplace, or becoming indifferent to being left with others
- Sexual awareness beyond what is age appropriate or what has been taught
- Inappropriate sexual behavior or play with other children
- Inappropriate childish behaviors or regression such as bedwetting and thumbsucking
- Aggressive behavior toward others
- Fearful of activities that were previously enjoyed, such as bathing, undressing, or playing somewhere or with someone

Notes

Chapter 1: What Is Sexual Addiction?

1. C. S. Lewis, in *A Mind Awake: An Anthology of C. S. Lewis*, Clyde S. Kilby ed. (New York: Harvest/Harcourt Brace Jovanovich, 1968), page 139.

Chapter 2: Sexually Addictive Behaviors

1. Patrick Carnes, *Don't Call It Love: Recovery From Sexual Addiction* (New York: Bantam Books, 1991), page 42.
2. Carnes, page 43.
3. Carnes, page 57.
4. Nicholson Bakker, *Vox* (New York: Random House, 1992), page 35.
5. Bakker, page 41.
6. Bakker, page 41.
7. Bakker, page 58.
8. Carnes, page 44.
9. See Exodus 22:19; Leviticus 18:23, 20:15.
10. Carnes, page 65.
11. Carnes, page 43.

Chapter 3: What Causes Sexual Addiction?

1. C. S. Lewis, *The Problem of Pain* (New York: Collier Books, 1962), page 115.
2. John Stott, *The Cross of Christ* (Downers Grove, IL: InterVarsity Press, 1986), page 109.

Chapter 4: Hope for Those Who Are Sexually Addicted

1. C. S. Lewis, in *A Mind Awake: An Anthology of C. S. Lewis*, Clyde S. Kilby ed. (New York: Harvest/Harcourt Brace Jovanovich, 1968), page 22.
2. Dr. Larry Crabb, *Inside Out* (Colorado Springs: NavPress, 1988), page 149.
3. See John 3:16 and chapter 20; Luke 23–24.
4. See Matthew 22:37-40, Luke 10:25-37, Romans 13:8-10.
5. C. S. Lewis, *The Voyage of the Dawn Treader* (New York: Collier Books, Macmillan Publishing Company, 1952), page 90.

Chapter 6: Preventing Sexual Addiction in Your Children

1. Kevin Huggins, *Parenting Adolescents* (Colorado Springs: NavPress, 1989), page 115.
2. Patrick Carnes, *Don't Call It Love: Recovery From Sexual Addiction* (New York: Bantam Books, 1991), page 109.
3. Quoted in *Colorado Springs Gazette Telegraph,* 15 March 1992, page D1.
4. Marry P. Koss, Christine A. Gidycz, and Nadine Wisniewski, "The Scope of Rape: Incidence and Prevalence of Sexual Aggression and Victimization in a National Sample of Higher Education Students," *Journal of Consulting and Clinical Psychology* 55, no. 2 (1987), page 162.

Chapter 7: Sexual Addiction in the Church

1. "How Common Is Pastoral Indiscretion?" *Leadership,* vol. IX, no. 1, winter 1988, pages 12-13.
2. See 1 Corinthians 6:13, Colossians 3:5, 1 Thessalonians 4:3, and Hebrews 13:4; Leviticus 18:6-18,23 and 1 Corinthians 6:9; 1 Corinthians 3:16 and 6:19; Proverbs 6:25, Colossians 3:5, and 1 John 2:16.

3. Dr. Larry Crabb, *Inside Out* (Colorado Springs: NavPress, 1988), page 36.
4. C. H. Spurgeon, *The Metropolitan Tabernacle Pulpit,* vol. XXXII (Pasadena, TX: Pilgrim Publications, 1974), page 398.
5. C. S. Lewis, *A Grief Observed* (New York: Seabury Press, 1961), pages 26-27,32.
6. Spurgeon, page 398.

Chapter 8: The Church as a Healing Community
1. Dr. Larry Crabb, *Inside Out* (Colorado Springs: NavPress, 1988), page 17.

Chapter 9: Healing for Christian Leaders
1. Reported by Dr. Arch Hart, Fuller Seminary, at the Care Givers Forum, Colorado Springs, Colorado, 1991.

Author

Dr. Harry W. Schaumburg received his M.A. from New York University, his M.S. from the University of Wisconsin-Milwaukee, and his D.Min. from New York Theological Seminary. Dr. Schaumburg is a graduate of the Center for Family Studies/Family Institute of Chicago at Northwestern University. He is a clinical member of the American Association for Marriage and Family Therapy and is licensed as a Marriage and Family Therapist by the state of Colorado.

Dr. Schaumburg is a therapist and speaker specializing in sexual addiction. He coauthored *Renew: Hope for Victims of Sexual Abuse* with Robert McGee (Rapha Publishing). Dr. Schaumburg has treated sexual abuse and sexual addiction for the past thirteen years in both private practice and in-patient settings. His current ministry is with Christian leaders and the problems of sexual misconduct and sexual addiction. He resides in Colorado Springs with his wife, Rosemary, and their two sons Aaron and Nathan.